heart of palms

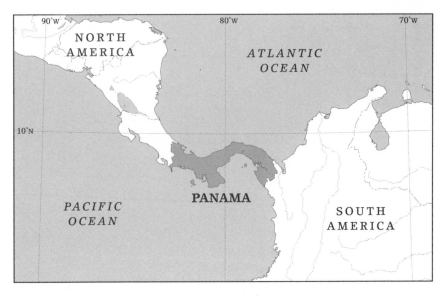

Map 1. Location of the Republic of Panama, linking two oceans and two continents. Map drawn by Matt Kania.

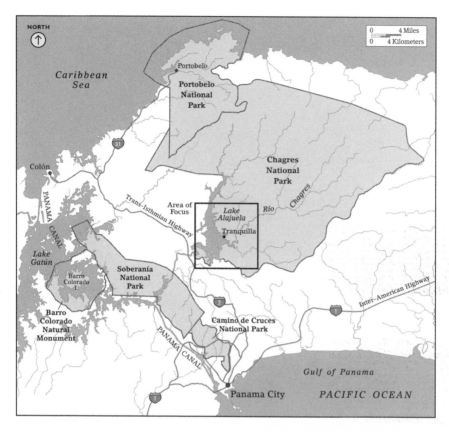

Map 2. Close-up look at the center of Panama, a nation divided into East and West by the human-made Panama Canal. Key sites mentioned in this book are all located within this central part of the country, including Chagres National Park, Lake Alajuela, and the village of Tranquilla. Map drawn by Matt Kania.

heart of palms

MY PEACE CORPS YEARS IN TRANQUILLA

MEREDITH W. CORNETT

Foreword by Florence Reed

THE UNIVERSITY OF ALABAMA PRESS

Tuscaloosa

Typeface: Minion and American Typewriter

Cover photograph: *View of Tranquilla on the shores of Lake Alajuela, 1992, by Ethan Perry*
Author photograph: *Chelsea Morgan, Magic Box Photography*
Cover design: *Michele Myatt Quinn*

∞

The paper on which this book is printed meets the minimum requirements of American National Standard for Information Sciences—Permanence of Paper for Printed Library Materials, ANSI Z39.48-1984.

Library of Congress Cataloging-in-Publication Data

Cornett, Meredith W., 1968–
    Heart of palms : my Peace Corps years in Tranquilla / Meredith W. Cornett; foreword by Florence Reed.
        pages cm
    Includes bibliographical references.
    ISBN 978-0-8173-1818-5 (hardcover : alkaline paper) — ISBN 978-0-8173-8740-2 (ebook)
        1. Cornett, Meredith W., 1968- 2. Rain forest ecology—Panama—History—20th century. 3. Rain forest ecology—Panama—San Vicente de la Tranquilla—History—20th century. 4. Women ecologists—Panama—Biography. 5. Peace Corps (U.S.)—Biography. 6. Americans—Panama—Biography. 7. Panama—Environmental conditions. 8. San Vicente de la Tranquilla (Panama)—Environmental conditions. 9. San Vicente de la Tranquilla (Panama)—Social life and customs. 10. San Vicente de la Tranquilla (Panama)—Biography. I. Title.
    QH108.P3C67 2014
    577.34097287—dc23
                                                                    2013029836

To Ethan, who was up for the adventure, and to Charlotte, who came along when we were ready for more.

Contents

Foreword by Florence Reed   xi

Acknowledgments   xv

Plant Species Mentioned in the Text   xvii

Introduction   1

PART I. SEED (GERMINATION): JULY–DECEMBER 1991

1. Armando   9

2. Plátano   15

3. Papaya   20

4. Teca   24

5. Exploración   27

6. Agua   31

7. Posadas   36

PART II. SEEDLING (TAKING ROOT): JANUARY–JUNE 1992

8. Brujería   43

9. Limón   47

10. Todo el Mundo   52

11. Acacia   59

12. Hormigas   67

13. Palmas   70

PART III. SAPLING (ESTABLISHMENT): JULY–DECEMBER 1992

14. Recursos Naturales   79

15. Donde el Gringo   84

16. La Operación   88

17. Victor Venenoso   92

18. Salud   95

19. Leucaena   102

20. Boa   107

PART IV. TREE (HARVEST): JANUARY–JUNE 1993

21. Demostración   115

22. Almejas   120

23. Quinceañera   123

24. Lorena   126

25. Miel   130

26. Bosque   135

27. Despedida   139

    Epilogue   142

    Resources   147

    Bibliography   151

Foreword

The honor of writing the foreword to *Heart of Palms* provides me with the happy opportunity to reflect on my treasured friendship with Meredith Cornett, the lessons we learned as Peace Corps Volunteers in rural Panamá, and how those lessons became the foundation of my present life's work. After we completed our Peace Corps service in 1993, I worked for a couple of different nonprofit organizations before founding Sustainable Harvest International (SHI) in 1997. SHI's mission is to provide farming families in Central America with the training and tools needed to restore our planet's tropical forests while overcoming poverty.

After working together every day of our three-month Peace Corps training in Costa Rica, Meredith and I each went off to our respective communities in Panamá, where we would spend the next two years of our lives. We were dropped into social and geographic landscapes that were equally foreign to us, but also quite different from each other. Yet we still worked toward the same ultimate goals and came away with similar lessons learned.

The community to which I had been assigned, Santa Rita, had been settled hundreds of years prior to my arrival. This had given the community time to bring a passable dirt road through the center of town along with electricity, running water, and a pay phone, all of which worked, some of the time. Families living away from the main road did not enjoy such luxuries of civilization but did benefit from hereditary rights to their land and the accompanying reassurance that any improvements they made were theirs in perpetuity.

The long history of Santa Rita and surrounding communities also meant that centuries of slash-and-burn farming, often followed by cattle grazing, had severely degraded the land. Almost the entire area was a patchwork of compacted baked clay devoid of topsoil, with little or no natural vegetation. Agricultural yields were understandably low and people were anxious to find an alternative that would continue to sustain their families. Some had already migrated to the city and, if they had been lucky, had found work that sustained their families physically, yet robbed them of the physical and mental health that comes from living close to the land and an extended family. Panamanians also went as far as the United States looking for better economic opportunities, which resulted in the fracturing of previously close-knit families.

Many of those who remained in Santa Rita worked with me to bring life back to the land by planting trees, but this was a long-term proposition and one I knew would have limited benefits if the cycle of slash-and-burn farming continued. Therefore, I created SHI to provide another alternative that could allow rural families to stay in their communities and produce enough from their land to sustain them for generations to come.

Since its founding in 1997, SHI has helped more than a thousand families become self-sufficient stewards of the environment by converting more than sixteen thousand acres of degraded land to diverse, sustainable, organic farm plots and by planting more than 3.2 million trees. It is gratifying to see these methods take root and spread. When we first surveyed families, years after they graduated from our program, we found that 100 percent continued to use what they had learned with us and had been sharing it with their neighbors.

I attribute the success of SHI's work in great part to a few key principles that grew from the lessons both Meredith and I learned as Peace Corps Volunteers. Probably the most important principle of this work is that it has to be long-term. Farmers cannot be expected to abandon techniques used for generations and switch to a more complicated farming system after a few weeks or even a few months of instruction. For this transition to take hold and flourish, years of regular technical assistance are required.

Second, a simplistic, cookie-cutter approach imposed from outside will rarely last. An integrated approach developed through conversations between program participants and SHI staff is essential for long-term changes in farming practices. Thus farmers bring their needs to the table along with their knowledge of the land, climate, and community. SHI staff members bring other knowledge, such as the long-term benefits of various organic practices and the destructive tendencies of repeated burning, use of agrochemicals, and loss of watersheds. The final core principle of SHI's work is the focus on local staff. It may be ironic that I learned this from the Peace Corps, but I could not help realizing how much more effective I could have been from the start if I had had a fuller grasp of the language, culture, and environment of Panamá. While Peace Corps Volunteers can get a lot done on the ground too, a local person will almost always be more effective.

Today, I still consider the Peace Corps to be extremely valuable for all it does in terms of building greater understanding between the United States and other countries while also creating US citizens who act as a bridge between their home communities and the broader world. For building national security and an informed citizenry, the Peace Corps is hard to beat.

In my role as founder and president of SHI, I spend much of my time trying to convey the importance and intricacies of SHI's work to many audiences. Over the years, I have found that nothing draws people in like a personal story, whether it is my story or the story of a farmer working with SHI. *Heart of Palms* seamlessly brings together a love story, a coming-of-age story, the stories of many rural Panamanians, and the story of one stage in a community's evolution.

Heart of Palms is a beautifully poetic rendering of many conversations I had with Meredith during our Peace Corps years. It brings alive a world few will know firsthand, while also bringing into focus the struggles and triumphs we experience in our own communities and within ourselves. Meredith's sensitivity to the people and environment around her shine through in her writing, with keen observations of the palm-filled world she inhabited in Panamá and her own heart of palms.

Florence Reed

Acknowledgments

First and foremost, I am grateful to the people of Tranquilla for helping me survive, tolerating my peculiar ways, and including me in their lives. To protect their privacy, the names of all people, and some details, have been changed. Most place names remain intact, as do the names of most—but not all—agencies and organizations.

Completing *Heart* never would have been possible without the understanding and support of my immediate family. Ethan Perry was the first to lay eyes on each and every draft. His editorial assistance, not to mention his help filling in memory gaps not covered by my own notes and journals, was invaluable. As far as our daughter is concerned, her mother has been working on "the book" for a lifetime. Many of these words were written with a newborn Charlotte snuggled against my heart, snoozing in a baby wrap. My own mother, Linda Bowdoin, was also an early reviewer of many chapters.

I have the good fortune of being part of a vibrant community of writers in northern Minnesota: Lake Superior Writers. The completion of this project is due in no small part to the practical advice, guidance, and support my fellow writers have so generously offered over the years. First among these is Mara Hart. My mentor of nearly a decade, Mara has helped me grow as a writer, applying her discerning editorial eye both to individual chapters and finally to the book as a whole. In addition, the members of Mara's Open Memoir Group offered frank critiques and encouragement as I brought drafts to share at our monthly meetings. The "Memoiristas," as I now call them, listened with attentiveness and patience. In particular, I thank Marty Bigalk, who often spent time between meetings providing more advice. Jill Hinners, one of the first to read the book proposal, helped me improve it in countless ways, and assured me of its potential. I thank Milan Kovacovic for the inspiration by example, and for being so generous as to read the manuscript in a time of extreme need. I also thank him for dispensing cookies to Charlotte, without which our visit might have been a disaster.

A number of friends made direct and practical contributions to *Heart*. Wendy Call gave advice through the lens of a friendship spanning four decades, as well as superb early editorial assistance. Matt Kania applied his artistic and cartographic talents to the maps and pushed the clock to finalize them in time for publication. Florence Reed, a genuine Peace Corps Superstar, wrote the foreword on a tight timeline in the midst of a demanding travel schedule. Adeline Wright sent me to a last-minute photo shoot looking much, much better than she found me—a true act of charity. Chelsea Morgan took that last-minute photo, proving once again that her "Box" is truly "Magic." My childhood friend, Claire Lewis Evans, kindled my initial interest in Peace Corps service and has fostered my creative life at critical junctures. Her quiet influence opened a second door when the first one closed.

Having written this book over a ten-year period, I feel tremendous gratitude for many, many other friends, family members, and colleagues. This circle keeps me in good health, good food, and good fun. For their friendship and understanding I especially thank Christine Douglas, Erica Hahn, Louise Levy, Jana Pastika, Kristin Snow, and Amy Westbrook.

I am grateful to the magazines that gave me the opportunity to share my work before finding a publisher for *Heart of Palms*. *LOST Magazine* was the first, publishing an earlier version of "Armando" under the title "The Life and Death of Señor Armando" (April 2009). *WSQ: Women's Studies Quarterly* followed soon after with the first appearance of "*La Operación*" (Spring/Summer 2010). I thank the *American Diversity Report* (editor, Deborah J. Levine), *Left Hand Waving* (editor, Dale Wisely), and *Dust and Fire* (editor, Maureen Gibbon) for publishing earlier versions of "*Posadas*," "*Hormigas*," and "*Brujería*," respectively.

Heart of Palms reflects only my personal views and should not be construed as a product of The Nature Conservancy. I am proud to be a scientist at The Nature Conservancy, one of the finest conservation organizations in the world. However, this book was completed on my own time.

Finally, I am eternally thankful to the University of Alabama Press for giving *Heart* a home. The day editor Elizabeth Motherwell called me at work was a turning point. Beth nurtured *Heart* from that day forward, helping me maintain my voice, stay true to my vision, and navigate the publication process. Her words: "Let's make a book!" We did.

Plant Species Mentioned in the Text

Native Trees

Albizia (Caribbean albizia) *Albizia niopoides*
Balo (quick stick) *Gliricidia sepium*
Corotú (false mahogany) *Enterolobium cyclocarpum*
Espavé (wild cashew) *Anacardium excelsum*
Guagara (broom palm) *Cryosophila warscewiczii*
Jira (stilt palm) *Socratea exorrhiza*
Membrillo (heaven lotus) *Gustavia superba*
Nance (golden spoon) *Byrsonima crassifolia*
Tagua (ivory-nut palm) *Phytelephas seemannii*

Introduced (nonnative) Trees

Acacia (black wattle) *Acacia mangium*
Gmelina (white beech) *Gmelina arborea*
Guayaba (guava) *Psidium guayava*
Leucaena (white lead tree) *Leucaena leucocephala*
Teca (teak) *Tectona grandis*

Fruit Trees (cultivars)

Limón (lemon) *Citrus limon*
Mango (mango) *Mangifera indica*
Naranja (orange) *Citrus sinensis*
Papaya (papaya) *Carica papaya*

Crops (herbs, vines, and shrubs)

Canavalia (jack bean) *Canavalia ensiformis*
Espinaca (vine spinach) *Basella alba*
Guandúl (pigeon pea) *Cajanus cajan*
Plátano (plantain) *Musa × paradisiaca*

Weeds

Paja mala/paja gringa (bad grass/gringo grass) *Saccharum spontaneum* heart of palms

Introduction

"The Idealism of the Peace Corps: Dead or Alive?" At age twelve, I had hoped that the bold title of my first term paper would mask an underlying anxiety over my new attempt at thematic writing. In researching the project, I had perused several Peace Corps brochures; I knew that the vaunted ideals of international service, friendship, and cultural exchange were alive and well. But I liked the doubt posed by my title and hung on to it even as the paper devolved into an exposition on Peace Corps history, the number of countries served, and the application process.

In truth, the Peace Corps's idealistic principles are constants that have spanned five decades since the program's inception in 1961. During his presidential campaign in 1960, then Senator John F. Kennedy proposed a "peace corps of talented men and women" who would apply their skills in developing nations around the world. Young people, mostly recent college students, responded enthusiastically to his call for service. Kennedy's vision was a direct response to the Cold War, creating an overseas service corps to compete with an existing Soviet program. Shortly after taking office, President Kennedy tapped Sargent Shriver, his own brother-in-law, to lead the task force that shaped the organization. On March 1, 1961, Kennedy issued the executive order that created the Peace Corps, with Shriver at the helm. Less than six months later, the first groups of Peace Corps Volunteers departed for Ghana and Tanganyika.

Long after turning in that report, I returned time and again to those first brochures. Each pamphlet sported images of attractive, wholesome-looking young Americans. They cultivated fields, built latrines, or planted trees. Adoring host-country children surrounded most of them, whether in a cement-block classroom, a church kitchen, or a pasture. Some of the Volunteers (in a Peace Corps context, "Volunteer" always has a capital V) were in native dress. I knew I had to join their glamorous ranks, or my life would have no meaning.

Of course, there was no way for me to know in 1978 that I would actually realize my dream of joining the Peace Corps and that my country of service would be the Republic of Panamá, where the dictator General Omar Torrijos had ordered the Peace Corps to leave in the early 1970s. I had yet to grasp that US foreign policy was the driving force behind the Peace Corps's placement of its Volunteers. The Peace Corps fantasy I had fallen in love with was a naïve mixture of adventure, romance, and good deeds.

Ten years later, other dreams had come and gone, but my desire to join the Peace Corps proved tenacious. In the spring of 1990, my senior year at Oberlin College, I found myself face-to-face with an on-campus Peace Corps recruiter. She was clearly pleased with my typed application and seemed unconcerned that I lacked any real skills. She assured me that with my impending bachelor's degree in biology, the Peace Corps could transform me into a forester, farmer, or science teacher. Surely I was "in."

Little did I know how arduous and drawn out the Peace Corps application and selection process can be. In my case, I endured a process that lasted as long as my actual Peace Corps assignment. The bumps and delays to which the Peace Corps subjects today's applicants are a true test of whether they have the patience for two years of service overseas.

My recruiters nearly lost me along the way. Despite my long-standing fervor for serving, I was having second thoughts about the Peace Corps by the time I received the offer. By this time, I was deeply in love with Ethan, a fellow student I had met during a semester abroad in Australia. Following college graduation, I worked for a summer at a marine laboratory in Mobile, Alabama. In the fall, I moved to Boston, where Ethan had picked out an apartment for us to share. He was finishing his senior year. I landed an internship at the Center for Plant Conservation, at the time located at Harvard University's Arnold Arboretum.

"Congratulations! You are heading to Panamá!" When the Peace Corps called with the long-awaited news, my mind conjured a squiggle-shaped country that I knew vaguely as the bridge between Central and South America. As the recruiter rattled off the departure and assignment details, I struggled to piece together the shreds of what "Panamá" called to mind: Hats. Canal. Noriega. Operation Just Cause. "This will all be explained in the packet you'll receive in the mail within a few days," he assured me. Thank goodness for that! I had hardly registered a word he had said.

I was honest with Ethan about my conflicting emotions. I could not imagine leaving him and the life we had just begun together. But I also could not envision a future that did not involve Peace Corps service. In the ensuing months before leaving for training, I worried I would be putting our relationship at risk. Ethan assured me that it would work out, and we made plans for him to visit Panamá six months into my service.

I would be one of only twelve new Peace Corps trainees to serve in Panamá following a nineteen-year hiatus from 1971 to 1990. Misgivings about serving in a country where the United States had so recently (1989) conducted a military intervention to depose a head of state weighed heavily on my conscience. Hundreds of Panamanians lost their lives when the United States invaded Panamá to oust General Manuel Noriega. Shortly after the United States installed Guillermo Endara as the new president, the Panamanian government invited the Peace Corps to return. I was acutely aware that the Peace Corps would not have been in the country at all had it not been for a military intervention that ensured a US-friendly government was in place. This was the Peace Corps's unseemly side, the likes of which I could not have envisioned as a ten-year-old. My relationship with the institution became more complex as it deepened. I ultimately decided to take the good with the bad and forge ahead.

Peace Corps Volunteers serving in Panamá in the 1960s had been focused on community development projects such as nutrition, livestock rearing, and basic sanitation. In contrast, our group was to work closely with the Panamanian government "to stem the tide of deforestation in the Panama Canal watershed." Panamá would be assuming control of the canal in the year 2000 and was concerned about the ramifications of slash-and-burn agriculture. Increased soil erosion and sedimentation could cripple the nation's major economic engine.

The day I first learned the name of the tiny village in rural Panamá that would be my home for two years, I nearly swooned: Tranquilla. Thanks to my nascent Spanish, I construed the name of the village to mean "tranquil," "calm," or "contented." Roughly translated, though, *tranquilla* means "trap," "hindrance," or "obstacle." Ignorance is bliss.

I further rejoiced to learn that Tranquilla was located within the 320,000-acre Chagres National Park. All the ingredients for a fairy-tale Peace Corps experience seemed to be in place. Little did I know that many of the challenges of my assignment would be directly attributable to the area's relatively new status as a park.

Only later did I learn that Tranquilla was in fact one of many small villages within the park. Although the term "paper park" was not yet in common use, the juxtaposition of human settlements and a supposed protected area struck me as odd. (A "paper park" is a park in name only, designated by statute, not in fact. It may show up on maps, but business-as-usual is taking place on the ground with little regard or even awareness of the protected area designation.) The incongruity mounted when I learned that the responsibility of enforcing park rules fell to exactly two park guards.

On my first visit to Tranquilla, during Peace Corps training, I was accompanied by two of my government counterparts—with the Institute of Renewable Natural Resources (INRENARE)—as well as my Peace Corps program director and a veteran Peace Corps Volunteer who had just finished serving two years in Honduras. We drove into Chagres National Park and took a motor boat across Lake Alajuela, where a storybook cluster of palm-thatched huts crowded the shore.

A throng of children met us at the boat landing, and a group of young men congregated around a ramshackle blue building that was pointed out to me as Tranquilla's only store. The men eyed me suspiciously as my INRENARE colleagues presumably explained that I was the new Peace Corps Volunteer, that my Spanish wasn't very good yet, and that I would need a place to live. They seemed to be vaguely expecting a volunteer, but certainly not a young blonde woman so seemingly lacking in skills.

It was immediately obvious that no one in Tranquilla would be able to pronounce my given name because of its awkward series of consonants, particularly the "th" sound at the end. I introduced myself as "Maria." A short man wearing a battered sombrero introduced himself as Patricio and offered to rent me a *rancho*, one of the palm-thatched huts, recently vacated by his son and family, who had moved to Panama City. He would charge a dollar per day for the ten-day site visit.

I scrounged enough food during the visit to get by, relying heavily on still-green mangoes from the communal trees, canned tuna, packets of crackers from the little store, and of course drop-in visits to neighbors at what I hoped would be mealtimes. I realized I needed a better plan to feed myself for my two-year stint, a more proactive approach that involved the right cookware and supplies. But I survived, and that was the point.

After our Peace Corps swearing-in ceremony and orientation week in Panama City, I set out again for Tranquilla. This time, I arrived without an entourage. A park guard dropped me off unceremoniously at Tranquilla's boat landing, and I disembarked with a backpack full of household essentials, a Peace Corps–issued medical kit, and a mosquito net. I dumped my things at the rancho I had rented during my site visit and went in search of Patricio, waving at a handful of onlookers and flashing what I hoped was a confident smile.

Patricio gave me a bulk discount. Over the next twenty-four months I would be spending a total of $240 on rent, or ten dollars per month. Now what?

I

Seed (Germination)
July–December 1991

1

Armando

I curse under my breath, waving an aluminum pot lid to revive a limp cook fire. The twigs and scraps of wood I scrounged from the margins of the village are too damp to do much more than smolder. The foulness of my language increases in proportion to my impatience. Just as I hurl the lid at the kitchen wall, someone clears his throat. Startled, I turn to find Armando Guerrel standing at my threshold.

Thank goodness I have been swearing exclusively in English, but how humiliating to have him witness my incompetence. I've been living in the village of Tranquilla for six weeks now, presenting myself as someone who will solve problems by planting trees. But all my neighbors have seen is a *gringa* (North American) who is struggling to feed and clothe herself.

"*Buenos* [good day], Maria," is all Armando says. I return the traditional greeting. To my relief, he saunters away.

Armando makes me nervous. A slight man of indeterminate age, he pops up wherever people gather. He materializes apparition-like at the church, skulks in the school's doorway, or entwines himself around a post at the store. Armando's individual appearances seemed peripheral to me at first, but his presence is central to the life of Tranquilla. His traditional rancho (thatched hut), a bedroom on stilts, crouches between the cooperative store and the Catholic church, a structural trinity that constitutes a downtown of sorts.

I give up on the fire and open a can of tuna, grabbing a dirty fork and eating straight from the can. Upon finishing the fish, I upend the can to down the remaining liquid. Tuna juice dribbles down my chin as I spy Armando staggering back up the path from my boat landing. He never seems to track quite straight. Now he carries a couple of massive logs and deposits them at my feet, where they inexplicably form a puddle.

"Oh! Where did you find those?" I try to sound casual.

"The lake."

Every dry season, skeletal tree trunks emerge from Lake Alajuela, dregs of the tropical forest flooded by the dam on the Chagres River in the early 1900s, when the Panama Canal was constructed. Villagers visit the ghost forest by *cayuco* (dugout canoe). They fell the remains of once imposing canopy trees, load the logs into their boats, and paddle them home. At the hearth, these last vestiges of the forest are split into shards for firewood.

Armando helps himself to my axe, and the splintering sounds of cracking wood fill the next few minutes. He neatly stacks enough firewood to last a week, if I am careful. I hand him a glass of lemonade, and he gulps it down, thanking me in the same breath. "*Gracias*, Maria." I fumble my thanks in return. He takes his leave.

That night, I dream I am working with several subsistence farmers to plant a few acres of upland rice on the lakeshore. To ensure the success of the planting, we extract a young man's heart and bury it in the center of the field. We mourn the brutal sacrifice but rejoice in the knowledge that it ensures a good harvest.

On waking, I am at first unable to shake the uneasiness of my dream. The feeling subsides as I boil water for coffee over a respectable flame. What a difference the right kind of firewood makes! I sit down and savor a sip.

When a few children from the village arrive, I am well into my second cup. They are here on official business and mumble hurriedly through their news. All I catch is something about Señor Armando and his canoe.

I ask the oldest girl to repeat herself; my imperfect grasp of Spanish often requires asking, "More slowly, please?" She looks at the ground and rushes through her short speech again. Something happened to Armando, but I cannot discern the details.

My tone harshens and I hiss, "*Qué le pasó a* [What happened to] Señor Armando?" They flinch, this time giving an answer that perhaps the gringa will like better.

"He is very sick."

"What?"

"He . . . died."

"What happened? Tell me!"

They find my hysteria off-putting and back away. *"Se murió."* They turn and run.

Señora Gabriela Castillo, Armando's sister-in-law, later passes through the village and stops at my house. She and a few others are on their way by motorboat to the larger town of Nuevo Vigia to fetch the authorities. She recounts the story for me.

The señora first caught sight of her brother-in-law's empty dugout canoe hovering across the bay from her rancho. She watched it all morning, but he never came back to retrieve it. She felt uneasy and commanded her oldest son, "Go fetch me Armando's boat before it drifts away." The youth paddled the short distance, grasped the tow rope, and felt an unexpected heaviness. He looked up and saw a bare, waterlogged foot wedged against the side of the boat. He drew back upon seeing his uncle, Armando, lying facedown in the water, draped lifeless over the side of his canoe.

After Señora Gabriela leaves, I keep to myself for the next few hours, staring at the fire. The wood Armando brought fades to coals, then ash by the time the villagers arrive with the police.

After a brief investigation, the police decide Armando died of natural causes. He had a long-standing heart condition and probably suffered a massive heart attack before landing in the water. The police remove the body to Nuevo Vigia, and several young men take a large cayuco to retrieve Armando's boat.

The forlorn little group returns to shore, the larger boat bearing the smaller one, like a mother loon ferrying a chick. Centaur-like, the people of Lake Alajuela are practically fused to their canoes. At the sight of Armando's vessel eternally separated from its owner, I surprise myself—and everyone else—by bursting into tears.

Gabriela takes charge of me. "But Maria, we must have the strength to carry on!"

I pull myself together, and we continue up the hill until we reach a neighbor's house. More mourners arrive, howling with grief. Armando's grandmother cannot stop screaming and throws a towel over her head. Her husband puts an arm around her and escorts her home. A brother-in-law weeps silently into the bandanna he still wears over his nose to dampen death's stench. These normally taciturn people cast away all reserve. I am frightened.

I flee to search for Gladys, Tranquilla's schoolteacher. Like many rural teachers, Gladys lives in Tranquilla during the week and returns home on weekends and breaks. Her husband and son live hours away in the province of Veraguas. I think she must be the only person in the village as lonely as I, but at least she speaks the language.

I find her at the school. She confides that she saw the body, hardly recognizable save for his clothing and boat. "I wish I had not seen it, Maria. You would not have recognized him. Now that I saw him, I always feel his eye on me."

Unsure I understood, I ask, "You mean Señor Armando's eye?"

"*El señor que murió*" (The man who died), she corrects me. I finally understand that the recently deceased are not to be mentioned aloud by name, not until the right prayers have been uttered the right number of times and in the right place.

Attended by her usual court of two or three girls from the school, Gladys prepares to take a sponge bath behind the privacy curtain that divides her living and sleeping spaces. "Will there be a Mass?" I want to know. The Belgian priest gives Mass in Tranquilla only once a month and it will be impossible to reach him in time.

"A prayer service. Tonight after sunset at el señor's house." Gladys herself will lead the service. One of the few people in the village not related by blood or marriage to Armando, Gladys is the closest thing Tranquilla has to a religious leader.

After supper, I join the others walking somberly to Armando's house. The soft glow of a dozen candles spills through the cracks of the palm bark walls. We pack into the tiny room, already purged of Armando's belongings, and sit with knees bent under our chins. The ceiling is so low, I realize he must have used the house only for sleeping. Always conscious of my height relative to Tranquilla's diminutive residents, I feel especially large in such close quarters.

Gladys slips into her role of leading the service. Her fingers creep along the rosary. She murmurs a spooky stream of prayer. The mourners are subdued now. Armando's brother sniffles throughout the vigil, head bowed more in sorrow than prayer. Gladys finishes with a last appeal, finally speaking his name: "May *el señor* Armando Martinez rest in peace."

"Guerrel," whispers a sister-in-law, correcting the surname.

"Guerrel, *disculpe*" (excuse me), apologizes Gladys. The spell is broken.

Several men are up all night making the coffin. The sounds of hammers and saws spin a heavy shroud around my thoughts as I lie awake for hours. The communal grief that has settled on the village is getting to me. Layers of isolation—from the world, from my family, from this grieving community—leave me questioning whether I can stick it out for two years.

The following day, in a sleep-deprived state of clarity, I send for someone to paddle me to Corotú, a ragamuffin port of sorts on the southern end of Lake Alajuela. Named after the giant *corotú* (false mahogany tree, *Enterolobium cyclocarpum*), which spreads its protective branches over the comings and goings of Chagres travelers, Corotú welcomes and bids farewell to all, though it does not appear on any map.

Just in case, I take my passport. Most folks barely take notice of my departure. Gabriela tells me to listen to Radio Mia, a national radio station, for the funeral time. The station has a daily, hour-long community messaging program filled exclusively with a reading of messages to scattered family and friends. For rural Panamanians, most lacking telephone and mail, Radio Mia is a vital public service.

"*Cómo no*" (Why not), I respond noncommittally.

Without much noticing the four-hour journey to Panama City, I arrive in a bewildered state at the Peace Corps office on Via España. The office is in the wealthy part of town, right across the street from Panama's only five-star hotel; the contrast with Tranquilla could not be greater.

"What, back already?" chides the receptionist as I walk through the lobby. I ignore the slight and head back to the Volunteer lounge seeking counsel, preferably in English. Luckily, two veteran Volunteers are in town on a supply run. I tell them about Armando, and Tranquilla's transformation around the death.

"What now?"

"Oh, don't worry about it," they assure me. "That's just a Latin American thing. They're really competitive about grief. It's sort of like, 'I can be sadder than you can,' chest thumping, that kind of thing."

As for death in general, one of them says darkly, "Get used to it. You're going to see a lot more of it." He lists all the deaths he has personally witnessed in his own village, the most awful of these a small boy by snakebite. I consider catching a taxi to the airport and hopping on the next plane home.

"I'm real sorry to hear about your friend," the other hastens to add. Her wistful, vague sympathy starts me thinking.

Was Armando my friend? Not really, although he leaves a palpable vacancy. Losing his ubiquitous presence is disorienting and unravels my nascent understanding of how the village functions. His death embodies change just when I was gaining a sense of the rhythm of daily life. How will the pieces reorganize? Will there be a place for me in the new configuration?

I tune the lounge radio to Radio Mia as instructed, the first time I have listened attentively to the program.

"Guillermo, this is to tell you that Mama and I will meet you this afternoon in Chilibre, God willing."

"Estela, return home at once. Jorge is sick and we need you here."

Finally I hear it. "The funeral of Señor Armando Guerrel will be held in Nuevo Vigia on Sunday at noon."

I spend the next day in town, pampering myself with an air-conditioned hotel room, CNN, and restaurant meals. I arrive in Nuevo Vigia late Sunday morning. By early afternoon there is still no sign of a funeral.

I return to Tranquilla in a hired cayuco, frustrated and confused. The smell of smoke greets my nostrils as I disembark. With a small crowd gathered at the store, I take in the charred remains of Armando's house. I gather that setting fire to the home of the deceased is standard practice, an elimination of the likeliest place for a ghost to lurk.

I unpack slowly. Someone stands again at my threshold. I turn and see Señora Catalina, my landlord's wife. Like Armando, she has a way of arriving noiselessly. We chat about the weather for a few minutes before I muster the courage to ask about the funeral. She explains, "We had to bury him last night. The body was just too far gone."

She has a parcel with her and unwraps it. She places a covered dish on the table. "Dinner. I thought you may not have had a chance to cook." The visit cheers me a little.

Armando's death briefly cracks the village apart. Over time, though, Tranquilla's broken bones mend together, closing around the gap he left. Villagers compensate for their loss in little ways. They adjust the schedule at the store, where Armando had been a primary clerk in the rotation. Each man works a little harder on cooperative projects. I gather my own firewood.

2

Plátano

A month has passed and I'm still adjusting to village life after Armando's death. I've spent my time *paseando* (visiting) with neighbors, trying to discern the store's nonexistent schedule, and dragging my atheist self to church.

Señor Patricio has taken pity on me by inviting me to join in a workday with the farmers' cooperative, the Unión Campesina del Lago Alajuela (UCLA, the Farmers' Union of Lake Alajuela). Today is the day, and I need breakfast.

The mangoes are still plentiful, many of them fully mature now, though the ones within my reach are just on the edge of ripening. I grab one from a tree in the backyard and peel the not-quite-ripe fruit with a not-quite-sharp kitchen knife. I hold the mango like corn-on-the-cob and nibble at it. My teeth shudder as they scrape the surface of its enormous seed.

I alternate between picking mango strands from my teeth and sipping tea. My stomach is slightly upset by the arrival of the stringy yellow-green contents. A ring around my mouth burns a little and I know a rash is forming. I recently learned that mango (*Mangifera indica*) is in the poison ivy family (Anacardiaceae). People sensitive to poison ivy also have a mild reaction to mangoes, especially greenish ones. That's me.

Not much of a breakfast, but it's time to go. I grab a dull machete left behind by the previous occupants of my rancho, pull on long pants and work boots, and walk over to Patricio's boat landing. He joins me in a few minutes and readies his cayuco. He paddles me to the field where the group will be working.

As he paddles, I try to make conversation in my halting Spanish. "Since how much time you have lived here in Tranquilla?"

Patricio tells me his family was among the first colonials to settle in the area, which was already dotted with a handful of indigenous villages. Almost twenty families make their homes in Tranquilla, scratching out a living on the steep hillsides surrounding the village. "When we came to Chagres, it was not a park," Patricio explained. "We left behind the barren hills of Coclé, in the interior. The spent soils could no longer feed us, so we moved on. This here seemed like the land of abundance."

When we arrive at the work site, about a dozen men have already partially cleared a field to sow *plátanos* (plantains, *Musa* × *paradisiaca*), a cousin of the banana and a staple served in soups and stews as *patacones* (fried green plantains). The men are battling an invasive exotic grass related to sugarcane. A formidable weed, this grass goes by many names, among them *paja gringa* (gringo grass), because it is rumored to have been imported originally by gringos to control erosion; *paja mala* (bad grass), because it is a scourge on the land; or simply *paja* for short. Paja (*Saccharum spontaneum*) rushes to fill a void, reclaiming every field cleared to plant corn or rice after only one or two seasons. A reproductive wonder, paja can sprout from the tiniest fragment, colonize by the tiniest seed.

Until today, this field was inaccessible, seized by the green sentry, fierce plumes of white fringe adorning an army of thousands. Today, we fight back.

We join the handful of others clearing the field, and I am immediately self-conscious. I tower over the assembled men, my fair skin and hair setting me apart, as usual. As I introduce myself to a few UCLA members I have not met yet, they eye me with suspicion, dressed as I am in long pants like a man. I wear boots where all the other workers go barefoot. No doubt they wonder what terrible thing I have done to cause my family to banish me for two years to a foreign land.

They give me a wide berth as I spastically wield my stub of a machete, my Spanish conversational skills as dull and clumsy as my implement. The men swing their machetes expertly. These barefoot farmers are so easy together as they move through their work. At first we work in silence. As the morning wears on, they gradually forget about me. Their bantering and *sala-mando*, a yodeling style unique to rural Panamá, pick up in earnest. Sala-mando is equal parts singing and barking and is meant to convey enthusiasm and general manliness.

Hard as bamboo, the paja is reluctant to fall. When it does, it actually clatters. We work all morning and fell paja stems across a field of about a hectare, two and a half football fields. Soon it will be too hot to work. I pause, lift the hair off the back of my neck, and fan myself with my hat. Toward the end of our labors, we stand on a thick, tangled mat of stalks and leaves.

Once all the stalks are laid horizontally, we make our way across the paja trampoline, which gives a slight spring to what would have been a trudge. We arrive at a nearby house, where we are welcomed for lunch by none other than Gabriela Castillo. I haven't seen her since that awful week when Armando died.

"*Buenos*, Señora Gabriela."

She looks me up and down, trousers, work boots, and all. Then a smile lights up her whole face.

"You can call me Gabi. Everyone else does, you know. I have been meaning to drop by, but I'm so busy here." She gestures to her many children, ten in all. She leads me to a steaming pot of boiled *yuca* (cassava), a root vegetable resembling a stringy potato, and piles a generous helping on a plastic plate. She hands it to me along with a fork, the tines of which are slightly bent. "Have a seat. You must be hungry."

She doesn't know the half of it. I feel downright lightheaded from hunger and heat. Although the yuca is still too hot to eat and it burns my lips and tongue, I am back for seconds before the others have even served themselves. The yuca is cooked to a bland mush but is by far the best food I've had in weeks. Gabi ladles the broth into mugs, which she passes around for us to share. Hot as the day is, the last thing I want is a steaming cup of starchy broth. But my head pounds with dehydration. Here goes. I sip tentatively and find she has added a little sugar. I savor it—thick, hot, sweet.

Lounging around Gabi's kitchen, I feel it is still too hot to work, too hot to move. Although there is no formal siesta in Tranquilla as far as I can tell, there is an unofficial "lazing" time that all observe. We do so lying around Gabi's compound.

The following day we return to the field to sow the plantains. Francisco, president of UCLA, arrives with two *motetes* (large baskets), piled high with plantain rhizomes, each of which will give rise to a new plant. The motetes are equipped with two straps. Fransisco lifts them one at a time from his cayuco, hoists them into backpack mode, and transports them to the cleared field. We sow the rhizomes in tight rows that should eventually shade out the paja. We use *coas* (long-handled, narrow spades) to coax the jumble of paja stalks aside and make a hole in the earth to receive each rhizome. This step goes quickly compared to clearing the field.

During the last half hour of planting, Gabi surprises me by joining us. She carries a coa of her own and wears a pair of trousers cut off at the knee. She is the only woman in the village I have seen wearing something even approximating work clothes. On the rare occasion that women do work in the fields, they wear what they always wear: modest knee-length skirts and short-sleeved blouses. Like the men, they almost always work barefoot.

We finish the planting. One by one, workers take their leave and head home to their families.

"Well, Maria, have a good evening. Are you sure you don't mind living in the village *solita* [all alone]?"

"I like my little rancho. But do you know a family I could eat lunch and dinner with for a few months?"

"I'll say something to Patricio's son-in-law before he leaves. That's him over there." She nods and points with her lips to a man in a bedraggled straw hat. "*Oye* [hey], Lorenzo!"

From the corner of my eye I see Gabi discussing something with the man—he and Patricio nod, shuffle, and look at the ground. Gabi waves and heads down the path for her rancho. I join Patricio and shake hands with Lorenzo. The three of us amble toward the *muelle* (boat landing). We pass UCLA's vegetable garden, and Patricio shows me around. Nothing is producing as it should. The tomatoes look weary, the peppers are riddled with holes, and the squash flowers sag. Everything gasps for water and nutrients.

Then, a yellowing vine catches Patricio's eye and he stoops to inspect it. He brightens upon finding two ripe cucumbers. He picks them, hands one to me, pulls out his machete and cuts an end off the other one. "They say this draws out the bitterness," he explains. I copy him. Lorenzo looks on, his eyes dark and inscrutable, set deep in their sockets. A right front gold tooth gives him the appearance of always smiling, although he rarely does so.

The three of us rub the ends of our cucumbers in circles until thick goo oozes forth. Holding the vegetable to my face, I inhale its northerly scent. We slice off thick rounds and chew them in silence, drinking them more than eating them. I savor the shimmery familiarity while Patricio and Lorenzo embark on a new taste adventure. Panamanian cuisine revolves around starch, often deep fried, with beans or fish making an occasional appearance. Green vegetables are a novelty, at least in rural areas.

Sharing a cucumber feels tangible, simple. I dread returning to my rancho to sit alone with my bleak thoughts until the sun sets and I start it all over again tomorrow. I want to linger in this cucumber moment as long as possible.

"Do you like it?" I finally ask.

"Not really. No flavor. Too many seeds."

We laugh.

I climb into the front of Patricio's cayuco. Patricio launches us and Lorenzo calls out, "Maria, I'll tell the señora you'll be eating lunch and dinner with our family starting tomorrow. One dollar per day!"

"Gracias, Señor Lorenzo! I'm very grateful. Until tomorrow."

"Until tomorrow, Maria!"

3

Papaya

I awaken to the monotonous coos of the pigeons, only a thin wall of *jira* (palm bark, *Socratea exorrhiza*) separating us. Charmed by these feathered creatures when I arrived in Tranquilla, I felt sure I would come to think of them as pets. In reality, they are meat birds, and until Patricio started renting to me, he and his wife treated this hut for months as a pigeon coop. When thought of a certain way, I suppose this hut remains a pigeon coop. So what does that make me?

There are around a dozen birds, give or take. Most are a pale gray with dark tails and wing bars. A dusky purple underscores the green sheen at their throats. If it weren't for the inexplicable warty thing at the base of each beak and the vacant look behind every orange eye, this bunch would look almost stately. With the exception of the three I call Larry, Moe, and Squab, it is difficult to differentiate them. I imagine this trio has a more distinguished lineage than the others. Their coloring is dominated by a rich auburn, pure in Larry's case. Moe has a white patch on the nape of his neck as well as a few tail feathers missing. Squab has a few white patches on his wings. Oh. Make that *her* wings. This becomes obvious when I catch Larry stalking her in an obvious attempt at courtship.

They strut around my kitchen, dining area, and porch, chests puffed. It is easy to support the "free range" concept until one's living space becomes the "range." I resent the time I spend cleaning up after these unsanitary birds, who leave droppings all over the floor and furniture.

Lying under my mosquito net this morning, I am startled by a couple of unseen birds that succumb to sudden and uncontrolled flapping, as they do several times a day. Let's face it. I do not love these pigeons. I will never love these pigeons.

I slip under the mosquito net and sit on the side of the bed. My bare feet cringe as they scrape the jagged floor of packed earth. Lately, mornings in Tranquilla have been hardest. I miss my friends and family the most when I wake to each formless day as a forestry extension agent without much to do. Most of all, I miss my boyfriend, Ethan.

After pulling on a shirt in the dim light of the rancho, I gaze upward at the pitched ceiling. The morning light shines through the thinning thatch of palm and thrusts a dusty beam into my darkness. Today is papaya day.

Patricio recently heard that gringos are willing to pay a good price for dried papaya (*Carica papaya*). The resident gringa, I confirmed this is the case, and a project was born.

My campesino neighbors know a thing or two about drying food for later consumption. Lake Alajuela is an artificial reservoir created to keep the Panama Canal operational during the dry season. The government stocks the lake with game fish like peacock bass (*sarjento*) and tropical bluegill (*vieja*). The farmers' cooperative built a low-tech solar dryer and started a small enterprise selling *seco salado* (dried and salted fish). Every month they catch a mess of fish and fillet them butterfly style. To preserve the fish for sale, the fillets are heavily salted and then dried on netting in a plastic greenhouse. The same process, minus the salt, should work for papayas. First, though, we need papaya trees.

I trundle the fifty yards past the school and down to the church kitchen, where an intergenerational group of about twenty has already assembled. From grandmas to toddlers, everyone has a job. A group in the corner fills uniform gray plastic planting bags provided by INRENARE. Plastic bags function as pots for those on a campesino budget. They greet me and I join them in scooping the rich, black potting soil.

I work alongside three-year-old Anita, Patricio's cherubic granddaughter. She stands barefoot in a pile of dirt, the colorful pattern of her dress smudged all over. Her stringy hair has mostly fallen out of its ponytail and she lisps, "Maria, why you here?"

"I'm working on papayas, just like you."

"Get dirty?" She eyes me doubtfully.

"That's all part of the fun. Can you top off my bag for me?"

She continues to stare, drooling a little. She scoops some potting soil into my bag. Some of it makes it in, but it takes a few tries.

"Will you deliver this to the girls, please?"

Anita clutches the bag with both hands and waddles carefully over to a gaggle of adolescent girls, who sow the seed. They whisper and giggle together, heads bent over their work. I join them, and silence ensues. Finally, Gabi's daughter mumbles a forced "*Buenas*, Maria."

I have obviously interrupted some choice gossip but stay long enough to run my fingers through the planting material. The seeds feel soft, dry, and fuzzy. It is hard to believe they are the caviar-like stuff that glistens in the salmon-colored cavity of a fresh, juicy papaya.

A few young men set about making a *semillero* (raised nursery bed). When the semillero is finally ready, smaller children shuttle filled bags, each with its precious cargo of papaya seed. Standing on tiptoes, the children carefully snuggle the plump plastic bags together and run back for more.

We pin our hopes on the tiny seeds. I imagine them already growing, vigorous and healthy, alongside the plantains in the cooperative field. When all the seeds are sown and the bags are in place, a few of the boys water the semillero by dipping perforated coffee cans into a big bucket of lake water.

After the seeds are sown and watered, I apprentice myself to the women preparing a group lunch. In the open-air kitchen of the church, we work our way through a mound of raw ingredients, whittling bunches of dirty, hairy root vegetables into gleaming, edible chunks. These we slide into a bubbling broth in a massive cauldron that rests on three large stones over an open fire. Someone sections a recently living chicken and slides the shimmering parts into the pot. Lunch is almost ready when we hear a motorboat in the distance.

The motor slows and putters into the boat landing. The crew sends a runner—a staffer from an environmental nonprofit—to the kitchen where we are gathered. He explains that the group is a bunch of gringos attending a conference in Panama City. They signed up for a reforestation development tour, and Tranquilla is the attraction. The afternoon downpour begins, and we are astonished to see the gringos scurrying up the hill, all fancy rain gear, notebooks, and cameras. Suddenly, they are in our grubby midst, each of them forming a separate puddle. We stare at each other in the relative shelter of palm thatching.

I smile proudly as Patricio describes the array of projects underway. In particular, he mentions the plantains and gestures toward the papaya nursery just completed this morning. Our guests take notes and snap photos, listening as an interpreter translates the main points. I am amazed that just months into my Peace Corps service, I identify more with the villagers, less with the tourists. Still, I half wish they would sweep me along into their evening, which is sure to include a restaurant meal, a glass of wine or two, a comfortable hotel room. The downpour lifts. The tourists head back to the city, underwhelmed.

It is getting late, and people pack up and drift home in little groups. The handful of us left behind discuss a watering schedule for the new nursery, but my heart is not in it. I am still slightly deflated by the gringos' departure. I join Lorenzo's family for a dinner of rice and fish, craving the closeness and ease of family life. Having followed virtually none of the dinner conversation, I head back to my rancho and turn on the radio.

I recently discovered the US Armed Forces Radio station. It broadcasts National Public Radio morning and evening news programs and has quickly become my most reliable daily connection with home. In fact, I am addicted, and it would not be a stretch to say I organize my whole day around radio programs. Tonight I hunch over the radio, greedily absorbing every word. When the news is over, I light the kerosene lantern and jot down a few notes in my journal. Although there is no mail delivery in Tranquilla, I scribble a long, lonely letter to Ethan. When I will actually get to the city to mail it is anyone's guess.

I hear a small "coo" and grab the lantern to peek around the corner of the house. The pigeons, eyes shut tight, are snuggled together on their roosting log. They are almost cute, and I envy the togetherness they take for granted. When it comes down to it, the pigeons have each other. I have no one.

4
Teca

My impatience builds as I wait for the INRENARE boat. It should have been here two hours ago. Despite my annoyance, when the boat finally arrives I all but bound, puppylike, down the hillside path to meet it. All dolled up in my boots, long pants, and new sombrero, I hope I look like a forester.

Román Diego, the superintendent of Chagres, greets me warmly. He introduces me to his colleagues: a statistician, also from INRENARE, and a forestry student from the University of Panamá. I haven't seen Román since my first visit to Tranquilla, and I fill him in on my activities. To the best of my linguistic ability I tell him about the plantains, the papayas, and the tourists. He listens until I run out of things to say, tells me that I have been very busy, and then describes the plan for today's work.

We will visit several overgrown *teca* (teak, *Tectona grandis*) plantations planted around twenty-five years ago. The plantations consist of little parcels, each smaller than a city block, scattered around the national park. Over the years, the plantations have been forgotten. They have not been properly thinned and today form a haphazard network of misshapen timber amid a patchwork of forest and pasture. Our job is to locate each one, take a few measurements, and assess their value.

Rain clouds blossom as we pull away from Tranquilla's shore. Before they picked me up, the group had already sampled one plantation in the nearby village of Victoriano Lorenzo. Now we take the motorboat toward the neighboring town of Quebrada Benitez. We will take measurements there and return to Tranquilla for the last plantation of the day.

As the first drops of rain fall, the statistician admonishes himself, revealing his dandified background in the process. "I forgot to bring a plastic bag to keep my wallet dry." By the time we reach Quebrada Benitez, my companions and I are drenched.

Inconsiderate or perhaps merely ignorant, the statistician and student plunge through the center of town. Barely aware of the residents raising their hands in greeting, they forge ahead to search for the plantation, engrossed in their own private conversation. Román and I stop to visit with a few households, explaining who we are and what our purpose is. The families we speak with seem puzzled as to our interest in the plantation but answer by jutting their chins in its general direction. "*Allá arriba*" (That's where you'll find it). We look up just in time to see our colleagues disappear into the forest in the opposite direction. We hastily excuse ourselves to retrieve them.

Entering the dank plantation is like descending the stairs to a dungeon. Young trees crowd together in quarters simply too small. Unlike the native tropical humid forests, this one is orderly and uniform by comparison, any chance for diversity suppressed by the dark squalor. We establish a square plot, twenty meters on a side. Román and I take diameter measurements for each tree in the plot, recording them as we go. The statistician trains his student to measure tree heights using a fancy new clinometer. They extend a meter tape from the base of each tree. The student learns to sight to the top of the tree, then to the bottom. He calls out the numbers and I add them together to get a total height.

As we take the motorboat back to Tranquilla, I reflect on these organic, mossy stands. Teak is native to southern and southeastern Asia but has been planted all over Latin America. I think of the rich wood in the dining room of my childhood home. I never before considered the origin of the wood in the modern table, matching chairs, buffet, and cabinets. Even now, it is hard to mentally connect the plantation we just assessed with furniture. When there were dozens of native hardwoods to choose from, why would Panamá import this one and plant it in a way that demanded intensive management to be marketable?

Once in Tranquilla, we stop at the store to buy a few snacks and gossip for a while with the shopkeeper. The statistician is absorbed in converting heights and diameters into volume estimates for the first two plantations and mercilessly re-counts each of his painstaking calculations. We are interested in his results, because each of the estimates could, theoretically, translate into dollars, depending on the current market value. However, my own enthusiasm wanes when the exchange between Román and the statistician makes it clear that the communities of Chagres National Park will not actually benefit directly from any proceeds related to plantation management. On the contrary, all profits will belong to the Panamanian government. But if local residents learn that trees have monetary value, maybe they will plant more of them. Or so the thinking goes.

We tromp across Tranquilla's baseball field toward the last plantation of the day, both punchier and more dispirited than we were at the start. To save time, the statistician lays the plot single-handedly, encircling our little group with bright pink pieces of flagging. Román and I work with the student on measuring diameters and heights. We call out numbers and the statistician records them from a comfortable spot at the base of one of the larger trees.

As we take the last measurements, I notice Román surveying the boundary of our plot. He is muttering.

"A side here. Here. Here. Here . . . and . . . *aquí*?"

With this observation, we all realize that in fact our "square" plot has five sides, not four.

"What kind of square is this, *hombre*?" Román bellows. He decides to laugh. Following his lead, we laugh, too. We call it a day and tacitly agree to pretend that the plot was after all a normal square, though our numbers make Tranquilla's stand look particularly well stocked. I pretend not to comprehend this part of the exercise and bid farewell to my colleagues before they head back to Panama City.

"*Que le vayan bien*" (May you go well on your journey).

From the looks of it, the teak plantations won't be providing a steady stream of income, to say the least. But it feels good to have done some real forestry for a change.

5

Exploración

My boss, Justin, visited last week and brought the mail. In addition to the packages from family, letters from friends, and back issues of *Newsweek*, the haul contained four new letters and a cassette tape from Ethan. The most recent letter confirms that he has his plane ticket and a visa and will arrive October 1, only a few weeks away.

I become a bundle of domestic energy. With a makeover, surely the rancho could resemble the palm-adorned paradise he has imagined these long months. I am motivated by my determination that Ethan will see me as a self-sufficient jungle woman, not the cowering gringa that has become my alter ego. I sweep away pigeon and chicken droppings, hang a hammock, and apply a fresh coating of ash to the stove—a gray-wash. The ash is a protective coating of sorts. One mixes ash with water to make a thick paste, then smears it over the whole stove and allows it to dry. This coating absorbs oil and other spills and can prevent chipping.

My clothes and shoes need serious attention. They have mildewed as the rainy season has worn on. The shoes can be wiped periodically, but the abhorrent stains cling stubbornly to my clothing. I scrub with the harshest detergent, soak them in bleach, and set them to dry in the sun.

Other preparations are needed to smooth Tranquilla's acceptance of Ethan. To facilitate things, I start telling everyone that *nos juntamos* (we are married) and refer to him as my *esposo* (husband). If ever questioned later on, I decide, I will just pass off any confusion as my poor grasp of Spanish from my early days. This is only an embellishment of the truth, I tell myself. After all, I do feel married to Ethan. We just haven't completed the paperwork. Yet.

We thought of serving together, but Peace Corps policy requires that couples be legally married at least six months before going overseas. Ethan decided to be a free agent instead. If he can find meaningful volunteer work in Panamá, who knows? Maybe he will stay for the duration.

When Ethan is finally in-country, we spend a few days in Panama City and then take an easy ferry ride to Taboga Island for a short beach vacation. We stay just one night, as Ethan is eager to see Tranquilla.

The bustle of the city falls away as we progress through the gauntlet of transportation that bears us back to Tranquilla. First we hopscotch from taxi to bus to bus to *chiva*. Chivas rattle over the Panamanian countryside hauling all manner of incongruous cargo. Seating consists for the most part of wooden benches lining the perimeter of the flatbed, with overflow on the laps of the bench sitters, the floor, the roof, the bumper, or hanging off the sides. On rare occasions, someone climbs up to the roof and hangs on for dear life. More often, bags and boxes are lashed up top. One or two seats are also available up front with the driver, a privilege generally reserved for the local schoolteachers and other minor royalty.

The last leg of our journey is by cayuco. Just prior to Ethan's arrival in Panamá, I bought the boat from Gabi's husband for forty dollars. It leaks a little but is basically sound and should last two years. Owning the boat thrills me in the same way getting a driver's license did at sixteen. After I buy secondhand paddles from a couple of neighbors for five dollars apiece, I am in business.

I am excited to show Ethan what life in my new village is all about, but also nervous that he will reject it—and me as well. To my relief, he is enthusiastic for the most part. He revives his college Spanish and introduces himself to Tranquilla as "Etan"—easier to pronounce without the *h*.

My last few months have centered on learning basic survival skills rather than on appreciating the natural environment. I am hesitant to explore on my own, and the concept of hiking for pleasure, just for the sake of moving one's body and taking in the scenery, is completely foreign to my campesino neighbors. The Peace Corps requires that every Volunteer sketch an evacuation map depicting the best site for a helicopter landing in case of a medical emergency. After such a sobering exercise I cannot shake the idea that danger lurks everywhere, in the form of a poisonous snake, an obscure jungle illness, a carelessly swung machete.

Accompanied exploration is a much better proposition. By land and by water, Tranquilla has much to offer semitrained naturalists. Several expeditions unfold over the next few weeks.

One pale, shiny morning, we push off in the cayuco and set about exploring the margins of the lake. We cruise up inlets, shallow of depth and sandy of bottom. We drag as much as paddle the canoe, soon abandoning the waterlogged vessel altogether. The water dazzles us and we get a good look at the bottom through its clarity.

A pebble catches my eye and I scoop it up. I gasp to find it is a perfect fossilized clam. Ridges radiate from its apex, and I imagine this spot millennia ago, submerged by an ancient ocean.

Next, Ethan notices an enticing bulge in the sand. He plunges his hand into the fine grains and extracts another treasure. A coil circles around an oblong structure and we puzzle out a snail shape. Flooded by oceans of the past and by the damming of the Chagres today, this spot will continue to experience the ebb and flow of the waters long after we are gone. All morning our fingertips examine lumps of smoothed limestone with mosaics of crescents, spheres, and rods mortared together—diatoms, roundworms, and fairy shrimp of another era.

We soon discover that Gladys, who is easily bored, frequently enlists her court of young girls to accompany her to one of the local swimming holes. The girls are forever drawn into her refined orbit of costume jewelry, lipstick, and high heels. Together they make these outings after school in the early afternoon, during the longest, hottest part of the day. They agree to include us in their next trip.

They in one dugout, Ethan and I in another, we paddle across the cove. On the far shore, we pick up a path of clay, smoothed by many barefoot travelers. The dense vegetation closes around us, and our nostrils take in the cool, moist air. Palms and ferns beckon as we relax into the deep, soft greens of the forest. We descend into a mossy draw, where the air is pure, cool refreshment. We must now ascend a natural ladder of craggy rock, black and slick. We leave our shoes at the bottom, abandoning them for a better grip.

Sharp edges of the gorge give way to smooth boulders, a welcome change to my bare feet. The children usher us to a wide pool and gesture to the small waterfall near an overhang. We float and tread water, our wet clothing billowing around us. We drape ourselves over rocks, chat, and giggle.

My ecstasy is diminished when I realize that Gladys brought with her a special shampoo to delouse the girls. Picking lice off one by one, she tosses them into the pool. I worry the evicted creatures will take refuge in my own mass of hair. We take turns showering under the falls and I rub a little of the shampoo on, just for good measure.

These jaunts offer Ethan and me chances for uninterrupted private time, a respite from village life. We reconnect in our shared love for the natural world, which is somehow all bound up in our love for each other. I had imagined being with Ethan forever but not necessarily having marriage be the vehicle for that long-term commitment. My ambivalence toward the institution of marriage was in no small part shaped by living through my own parents' divorce. But although I am still by and large too young, anti-marriage, and emotionally underdeveloped, I find myself asking Ethan what he thinks about getting married after all. To me. We are alone in the back of a chiva, of all places. And no, I tell him, I am not proposing to him, just kind of starting a hypothetical conversation.

Ethan takes a little longer than I would like but responds with, "Well, I guess I'm not totally opposed. But I have to think through some things before we pick this back up."

We love getting out and about together, but Ethan also needs his own time and space, and his own way of connecting with nature privately. Near the teak plantation lies an inviting stretch of rolling terrain. Every so often he wanders that way with a machete. He hacks away at a little more of the forest each time to open a trail into the *monte* (scrubland). Like a parting of the sea, it tends to fill quickly behind him.

Naturally, I worry. What about snakes? What if Ethan cuts himself and bleeds to death?

"What if you get lost?" I finally say out loud.

He smiles. "That's the whole point of making a trail. I can always find my way back to you."

We kiss. "Be back before dark" is what I say. *I hope you'll always want to find your way back to me* is what I think.

"So maybe we could."

"Could what?" I'd spaced out the marriage conversation already.

"Try getting married."

"Try?"

"We might like it." He kisses me again and strides across the commons, machete slung over his shoulder.

6

Agua

A few weeks later, Ethan swings a pickaxe high over his head. It slides through the crusted earth with surprising ease but stubbornly resists his attempt to lift it again. As he works it back and forth, a small geyser shoots from the parched earth and into the air. He is dumbfounded.

The specter of Señora Catalina flashes before me. Just after I moved into the rancho, she gave me an orientation to the pigeons, furnishings, and yard. Although open to my gardening plans, she emphatically pointed out the location of the water main.

"Do not ever dig in this spot." She gestured to the spot where Ethan and I now stand. "If you do, you will cut off the water supply for the entire village."

At the time, my Spanish was shaky, my brain saturated with new information on survival and social customs. Like so much crucial information, the location of the water main scurried off to some dusty cupboard of my mind and remained hidden. Until today.

The day had started like any other. We sat at the table, mugs of coffee in hand, reminiscing and giggling over our families' reactions to our marriage news. We called them on a recent trip into the city.

"Oh! Why?!?!" was my mother's response. She's in the midst of her third marriage and is leaning toward thinking it may not be worth it.

"Well. You proved a lot of people wrong," Ethan's father offered. Hmmmm. We're not sure what they were wrong about. We didn't ask.

"It's about time! Your grandparents will be so relieved! You know how they feel about you two living together like that," my aunt told me. Actually, my grandparents never told me that they disapproved of our living arrangement, but I guess now we know.

"I'm going to be an aunt!" exclaimed Ethan's little sister. She's putting the cart before the horse in a big way, and it's not clear if she assumes I'm already knocked up or if she just figures we'll start having babies right away.

In any event, we're excited, we're nervous, and we're ready. We think. But here it is November, we won't be tying the knot until my mother visits in February, and we need to occupy ourselves today.

We decide to transplant fruit trees. I started them from seeds shortly after arriving in Tranquilla. Many of the seedlings are already big enough to move on to their next life stage. We will move the seedlings from my small semillero to new homes in plastic bags. We used all the gray INRENARE bags on the papaya project, but for months I have been hoarding plastic bags from the purchases of rice, beans, and other staples for just this purpose.

Satisfied with this plan, we sip the last of our coffee, snatching views of Lake Alajuela through the trees. The first hint of a breeze feathers across our faces, signaling that our leisurely morning will now segue to working in the garden.

We have a little of everything: *gmelina* (white beech, *Gmelina arborea*), oranges (*Citrus sinensis*), lemons (*Citrus limon*), papaya, and even breadfruit (*Artocarpus altilis*). Surely something in our green menagerie will convince our neighbors that tree planting is useful to everyday lives, not just to the environment.

The tropics are famous for poor soil. Unlike the abundant lake clays, soil rich enough to nourish young trees is hard to come by. Early in my Peace Corps career, I aimed to supplement the depauperate clay with homemade compost. That idea lasted as long as it took me to notice my neighbor's free-roaming chickens eating the household scraps faster than you can say "rot."

In addition to lacking nutrients, the ground, beyond thirsty, has descended into a delirium from prolonged dehydration. Dried to the consistency of concrete, the clay has contracted and pulled away from itself. Navigation through the maze of cracks zigging and zagging across the village commons has become increasingly difficult. The casual soccer and softball games organized during much of the year have now been abandoned, given the hazard. The chasms yawn menacingly, as if threatening to swallow small children and dogs, or at least devour a foot up to the ankle.

Where, then, to find soil to fill the planting bags? If we were in the United States, we would just hop in the car and run to the garden center for bagged potting soil. But we aren't, and we can't, so we turn to our own yard, which measures about one acre. Our landlord maintains the lawn encircling the rancho. Underbrush and yuca grow on the outskirts. On the theory that the lush plant growth may have softened the soil and enhanced its fertility, we select a spot near the fence shared with the adjoining property.

It is on this spot where we now stand. I try to convey to Ethan the gravity of the situation. We weigh our options and think of judgment day before the Water Commission.

The commission is made up of the same community members as all the other committees: Tranquilla's dozen or so adult males and a handful of women. The UCLA, the *Padres de la Escuela* (Parents of the School), the cooperative store—all adults must fill all roles. This in an undernourished community whose members barely have the energy to farm their desperate plots.

Ironically, Tranquilla, surrounded by the waters of Alajuela, did not have safe drinking water until a few years ago. I pay the commission one dollar per month for the luxury of running water dispensed from a single tap outside my kitchen. I have seen the source only once, a small stream harnessed to fill an enormous water tank. The tank sits at a higher elevation than the village, and gravity pulls the water down to the homes. Unlike many so-called rural development projects, it has worked perfectly. Until now.

Through lengths of PVC tubing stitched together with plastic joints and glue, the potable water journeys to our little peninsula. When the lake level is high, during the rainy season, the drinkable water flows protected through the undrinkable brew of lake water. During the dry season, when the lake is low, canoes pass under the plastic pipes as if they were telephone or electrical wires casually strung overhead.

Once it reaches the village proper, the water continues its journey underground. In the tropics, water pipes do not have to be buried deeply; there is no worry about frost heaves or burst, frozen pipes. In fact, so important is the pipe and so well known that there is no worry of damaging it. That is, until a couple of half-witted gringos set up housekeeping in your village. In that case, as we have just demonstrated, there is a great deal to worry about.

Utterly panicked, I decide we must go house to house to alert people to the problem. Ethan and I split up the route and we each sprint for the first house on our list. My first stop is our next-door neighbor's. She is deaf. Using a combination of hand gestures and filling a bucket at her faucet, I take several minutes to communicate my message. All I can think of is how quickly water is draining from the tank and how I need to notify a dozen other households.

Finally, understanding shows in her face. She gasps and exclaims, "El agua!"

I nod and yell "Sí! Sí!" over my shoulder as I flee to the next house, that of Señor Lorenzo. The parents are nowhere to be found, but I holler to the kids that they should quickly fill as many buckets with water as they can. No one is home at Señor Patricio's, either, and I fill a couple of buckets for his household.

It goes on like this for a while, and I remember that everyone is attending a special service at the Catholic church in the neighboring village of Victoriano Lorenzo. I find one empty house after another, and my biggest fear looks likely to materialize. Not only will we have to shut down the water for repairs, but before we can do so, the water will hemorrhage through the wounded line and the tank will empty.

Finally, I knock at Señor Tomás's house. I wait several minutes and almost give up, but apparently he has been napping. He staggers, blinking, to the door. Once my panic registers with him, he sets some water aside and then, saying he does not know how to turn off the water at the source himself, strides down to the muelle to get his cayuco and makes speed for Victoriano Lorenzo, where the church service is. When Tomás returns with one of the Water Commission members, the two men hasten up the hill to the water tank. They save about a quarter of the supply.

The commission is uncharacteristically efficient about the repairs. The following day, several members travel to nearby Nuevo Vigia and purchase extra tubing and joint compound. The next morning, two commission members are on the job at our house before Ethan and I are even out of bed. I put the coffee on and fry up patacones and yuca to offer by way of apology. Taking a break, each man silently accepts the refreshment, glancing every so often at each other, but never at us. Whether they are upset, trying to avoid embarrassing us further, or simply in a standoffish mood, I'll never know.

In all, the village is without water for only two days while repairs are underway. Meanwhile, the little stream slowly trickles into the holding tank, replenishing what drained away. A few weeks later, I attend the next commission meeting, pay my delinquent bills, and cover the costs of the repairs, about ten dollars in all.

I am relieved to absorb the potshots and jokes that are now possible with the passage of time. "Gringos. When they do something, they go all out," offers Señor Patricio. "Hey, Maria, next time you and Etan want an extra tap at your place, come to us. No need to go making your own like that," follows Señor Lorenzo, his gold tooth gleaming within the mischievous smile he cannot suppress. And on and on. The incident transitions from egregious wrongdoing to folkloric entertainment. It wraps around me, becoming part of my identity, the collection of shared experiences finally shaping a space of my own within Tranquilla.

7

Posadas

Several weeks later, Ethan and I crowd together on a wooden bench at a neighbor's to observe the first night of Las Posadas (The Inns/Lodgings). Including Christmas Eve, Las Posadas takes place over nine consecutive nights. Each night at dusk, would-be pilgrims make a small procession to a different home. The celebration is a loose reenactment of Mary and Joseph's trip to Bethlehem, although the resemblance seems a little tenuous. The hosts meet the group at the threshold and pose as innkeepers. A perfunctory role-play ensues with general agreement that there is no room at the inn. At this point in the exchange, the visitors are ushered inside.

By the light of a single candle, Señor Patricio reads aloud from a mimeographed book of Christmas prayers. Apart from Gladys, Patricio is the only resident of Tranquilla with both the ability to read and the confident authority to carry off a religious service.

Ethan and I are nonbelievers, but there are only so many nightlife options available in Tranquilla. We therefore participate in Las Posadas with enthusiasm, at least at first. Each night is a slight variation on the last: a few carols, prayer and sharing, light refreshments. Truth be told, the festivities are a little lackluster, but we do our best. The carols are the most difficult part. No one really knows them, nor do they really want to sing. The group tries to compensate by clapping vigorously, but this only makes things worse. We soon lose focus and our attempt dissolves into a few arrhythmic slaps.

By this time, Señor Patricio decides to move on. He leads us in a few responsive readings and then announces our discussion theme for the evening: the role Jesus plays in each of our lives. Patricio is an anomaly in Tranquilla, with his reading abilities and motivation to probe deeply into spiritual matters. An awkward silence ensues. Even the darkness cannot conceal his expectant expression as he swivels his head to look from one person to the next, waiting for a reaction. Poor Patricio. Rural Panamanians are just not given to discussing their feelings publicly on any topic, much less their personal relationships with Jesus Christ.

In the absence of a true volunteer, Señor Patricio puts my Ethan on the spot. "And what does Jesus's birth mean to you?" Ethan's dusty college Spanish is not yet fully revived, and it seems unfair to single him out like this. Even in English he has surely never given the Jesus matter a second thought. What will he do? Give a remedial explanation of the manger scene?

He uses the language barrier to his advantage and responds as if the question were "What does the holiday season mean to you?" Ethan launches into a halting explanation of his disdain for the commercialization of Christmas. The translation goes something like this:

"Corporations seize holiday? Commercialism bad, better peace on earth. Simple. Celebrate birthday of Jesus, never plastic crap."

Everyone relaxes, their relief palpable as Patricio picks up on Ethan's thread. He heartily agrees and even elaborates, noting that Christmas in Panama City is about materialism. In contrast, "Here everything is about community, family. We have the real thing in Tranquilla, no?" We are aglow with gratitude for Ethan's performance, realizing that the pressure is off—at least until tomorrow night's Posadas.

In the last few days before Christmas, scraps of everyday life are stitched together to approximate holiday decorations, but it seems a tremendous effort. In one household, a tattered red bandanna brightens a makeshift nativity scene. In another, a wisp of tinsel stretches across the deteriorating thatch of palm. A one-armed plastic Santa dangles from the awning of the village store, his beard gone beige from years of weathering.

Ethan and I make cards for friends and family in the evenings using scrap paper and paints to create tropical Christmas scenes of various kinds. We realize the cards will be late, but we should be able to mail them when we travel to Panama City around the New Year, and we want to spread the news about our February wedding to our combined list of friends and family. We leave our first batch of cards on the table to dry overnight and then turn in.

The next morning, I check the cards and am bewildered to find them blank. "What the . . ." Then I see the droppings. A gigantic cockroach scurries off the side of the table. "Gross! The cockroaches ate the paint!" After that, we decide to work on the cards earlier in the day, so the paint can dry before sunset. Each night we store the new cards inside a ziplock bag for protection until we can mail them.

On Christmas Eve, an assembly line forms in the open-air church kitchen to make tamales. A pile of freshly harvested sweet corn waits in a corner. An old woman pours clean kernels into a meat grinder clamped to a wooden table, and a starchy yellow paste oozes from the bottom and slumps into a plastic washtub.

Meanwhile, several men work with the outermost leaves of the husks to craft tamale wrappers. It looks as if they are shucking corn. Heck, we know how to do that! Ethan and I pull up chairs and rip at husks with abandon, tossing them into a bin for waste. One of the elders clucks and intervenes. He shows us how to separate the leaves from the base with a delicate slice of a sharp blade. Following his example, we choose the best of the leaves, place them carefully aside, and move on to the next ear.

A teenage girl shows me the next step. She spoons up a little corn paste and then swaddles it with a wrapper—a fold here, a tuck there, and we soon have a tidy bundle. She ties the package with a narrow strip of husk to hold it together in the boiling water. I repeat this process in a satisfied, meditative state. Making tamales is part food preparation, part craft project.

An impressive stack of tamales is ready for boiling in the large kettle over an open fire. The lead cook adds them to the kettle and puts a lid on top. Their delicate scent rouses my appetite, but we make batch after batch before tasting them. Finally, the work is done and the feasting begins. I relish the delicate sweetness of the tamales and eat them as quickly as they are placed before me. Although the tamales are surprisingly dense—their texture resembles that of an extra-moist pound cake—we gobble at least a half dozen each.

Everyone eats, visits, eats some more, and cleans up. We are swept away to midnight Mass, what all the Posadas have been building toward. Patricio and a handful of other recruits mumble their way through the service. After about an hour, I am dismayed to realize the Mass is sort of a mega-Posada, which shows no sign of letting up. Ethan and I struggle to stay awake.

The church is eerie in the glow of the candlelight. I watch the play of flames and shadows along cracks in the stucco walls. Ethan finally succumbs to sleep, and I burn with envy. I notice some of the community youth lurking in the margins of darkness outside the church. How I wish I could trade places with them, free to leave undetected at any time.

At the height of the manger pageant, Ethan jerks awake to the piercing cries of Tranquilla's youngest citizen, a six-month-old who has been recruited to play the baby Jesus. Baby Jesus is evidently grumpy about this turn of affairs and howls for the remainder of Mass. We are grateful when the whole thing is over and we can go to bed.

We awaken a few hours later to the sound of drums. Although curious, we feel burned out on village life and resolve to hold the village at arm's length today. We pick our way to the top of the hill behind our rancho and peer over it to catch a glimpse of the latest festivities, taking great care to steer clear of the celebrants.

A procession to the church is in full swing. Children wind their way across the village commons toward the church. Woven fronds of palm arch over each length of their route, adorned with a profusion of bright red hibiscus flowers. Many in the procession carry banners, also crudely fashioned of palm. An older boy brings up the rear, shouldering a rough-hewn cross as big as himself. All disappear into the church for yet another service.

We leave Tranquilla to its revelry and slink into our rancho for an American-style Christmas, more or less. We indulge ourselves in a day of hedonistic privacy. Our families in the United States had sent boxes of utilitarian gifts they hope will make our lives easier. We are delighted to find a solar shower, collapsible plastic containers for storing drinking water, and long-sleeved work shirts. There are even a few luxury items—board games, a glittery silver mobile in the shape of stars and a moon, and several pounds of M&Ms.

We keep to ourselves, greedily hoarding these items. We gobble chocolate, play games, and listen to Christmas carols on the Armed Forces Radio station. Rejecting materialism was nice and all during Posadas, but today we embrace it and give our tacit thanks to the corporations that usurped the Christmas season.

Around dinnertime, we hear a tentative knock at the door. We don't answer but hide our treats just in case we are discovered. The knock again, and a child's voice asks, "Maria? *Están aquí* [Are you two there]?"

If we are perfectly still, maybe she'll think we are asleep. When we are sure the child is gone, we peek outside at our porch. On the table sits a pot, with a generous helping of rice with chicken. It is still warm. While we were busy protecting what was ours, our neighbors went out of their way to share with us. No room at the inn, indeed.

II

Seedling (Taking Root)
January–June 1992

8

Brujería

My afternoons are lonely these days. Some American embassy friends helped Ethan find a primo volunteer position with the Smithsonian Tropical Research Institute outpost on Barro Colorado Island. It's a great opportunity for him, and he loves the work. But it's an adjustment. I'd grown accustomed to having Ethan with me again. Barro Colorado is a few hours away by chiva, bus, and ferry. He left Monday morning and will be away all week.

"Maria!" quavers a vague voice. Juana.

I cringe with the realization that Juana has succeeded in finding me home alone. What if she corners me here all afternoon? Whether I'm lonely or not, this is not exactly the company I have been wishing for.

Since arriving in Tranquilla, I have tried in earnest to appreciate Juana as a mere eccentric. Still, a mild horror seizes me as I watch her limp to my rancho. Juana is toothless and mangy, in rapid decline due to drink and age, but she often sizes things up with a surprising clarity. Conversations with Juana flit between the outlandish and the mundane.

"I returned the day before yesterday. And how is your hand?" she croons. "They tell me you have a *granito* [a sore]."

I start to show her the lump that recently appeared on my wrist, but common sense prevails. She fancies herself to be a Chocoe-Emberá tribal medicine woman. However, I have seen the festering results of her medical interventions, performed mostly on the neighbors' children and pets. Hastily assuring her that I am already much better, I back away to leave for the store, the school, anywhere but here.

"And Maria, when will you have *un bebé*?"

"Not for a long time, señora. When I return to my country."

"Oh, you are going, Maria. You are going." She shakes her head sorrowfully.

"I have more than one year left here in Panamá. Then I return to my country by bus."

"Ah. You have been here a year. You have one more year. And after that, you return to your own location." She slurs. "You will have two years here. When you return, you'll return badly, I tell you!"

I do not know, nor do I wish to ask, what Juana means.

She nods and peers at the thinning palm thatch of my roof. "And this house, does it rain?" I explain that the palm thatching has a few leaks, but nothing major.

Her gaze now settles on the row of tin cans on an upper shelf above my table. "Do all those cans have *leche* [milk]?" she asks, wide-eyed.

"No. They did, but now there is no more."

"That's a lot of milk, Maria! That's why you're so fat!"

I am ready to wrap up our chat. She lingers and then asks if I have mangoes. I point to one of the branches that still has a few small fruits.

"When will we see each other again?"

"Oh, sometime," I reply, not wanting to encourage her.

"I will not be here tomorrow!" she screeches. "I will be going to shell clams!"

I excuse myself, saying that I must run to Señor Patricio's with the rent money, a legitimate excuse, but one I invented on the spot. I leave Juana to fend for herself and pray that she decides to bother someone else before I return.

Patricio and Catelina have the fanciest house in the village. At the center looms a massive beehive oven fashioned of cement and local clay. Señor Patricio supplies the entire village with bread, baked a few times a week and sold at the *tienda* (store). Never mind that the little *pancitas* (rolls) most resemble glorified hot dog buns; they are bread where before there was none.

Patricio also owns the only refrigerator in Tranquilla. Powered by kerosene, the contraption pays for itself through the sale of cold Coca-Cola (twenty-five cents each) and *duros* (literally, "hards"), homemade popsicles of pineapple, lemon, or orange (ten cents each).

To celebrate my successful escape from Juana, I hand Señor Patricio a quarter and settle in to enjoy a cold Coke as day fades to evening. We chat amiably, and I pay him the ten dollars for that month's rent. After almost half a year in Tranquilla, it finally feels comfortable and natural to pass the time casually.

Patricio's daughter and granddaughter soon join us. A frenzied chatter erupts, an intrusion on the easiness of our conversation. I desperately snatch at conversational fragments, losing one as quickly as I try to piece it together with the last. With some difficulty, I conclude they are discussing a recent outbreak of *brujería* (witchcraft) in the village and surrounding area. Among their accounts: a teenager becomes disoriented in the morning fog while paddling to a neighboring village and blames *brujas* (witches) for blowing him off course; the caretaker of a nearby *finca* (estate) reports that a *bruja* has braided his mare's tail every night for the last week; up the Chagres River, an elderly Chocoe woman is accused of putting a curse on a neighbor, who in due course nearly dies of excessive menstrual bleeding.

As the women simmer down, Señor Patricio, perhaps sensing my plight, tells a story at a slow, deliberate pace. A while back, he awoke in the night to the sensation of something tugging on his sleeve. It happened to be Halloween, *La Noche de las Brujas* (The Night of the Witches), as it is known in Panamá. He jumped out of bed and chased the presumed phantom into the kitchen, where it flew away.

"Sí," agrees his daughter. "When they behave like that, they are trying to forget what it is they have learned." She makes this pronouncement with such authority and conviction that I almost forget to be confused by its ambiguity.

Señor Patricio asks if I have any experience with witches. Is this a trick question? Perhaps he is just politely trying to include me in the conversation. In such a superstitious community, however, there may be serious consequences to admitting any familiarity with brujas or brujería. I deny having any knowledge on the subject.

He nods understandingly. "There are some that they pursue more than others, and I am one of those pursued. A witch is a woman, any woman, who comes in the night and sucks the blood of human beings. She is weak, because she is in contact with the Devil, who in turn is feeding on her. When she comes, you must remove all your clothes, and put them on again, but inside out."

I bid the group good-night and pick my way home through the gathering darkness, marveling at the absurdity of their superstitions. But let's face it. Village life is ever the same dull story, and in Tranquilla the fodder for gossip is limited to a dozen households. Legends of witchcraft offer an imaginative escape.

The slope of the earth signals that I have nearly arrived at my hut. A creepy

feeling overcomes me as I make out the barest hint of a human shape standing in my kitchen, and I remember Juana. I swallow a gasp just as I realize
no one is there.

Normally, I relish my solitude. Tonight, though, I shudder as the question villagers frequently ask replays in my mind. "Does it not bother you to
sleep here *solita* [all alone]?"

I light a fire to warm some rice for supper. I thrill to the ritual and imagine
the flame driving away unwanted spirits and witches, Juana included. Chuck-
ling, I admit to myself that I share the credulous nature of my neighbors.

9

Limón

The sun-soaked path ahead is awash in blurry blue. A formation of twirling splotches hovers above the trail. At first I mistake the shapes for pinwheels. Now I see they are makeshift ornaments draped over the bones of a scrappy lemon tree. Stunted and nearly leafless, the lemon shivers in the heat. My God, it must be at least ninety degrees and it's only midmorning.

One-quart boxes of milk—gifts from the Panamanian government—were distributed by the case to the poorest rural citizens over Christmas of 1991. Now empty, the blue boxes have taken up a second career. I grab one to inspect it. The carton is carefully slatted, compressed slightly to allow the slats to balloon out, and suspended from a fraying string. In the transformation from carton to whirligig, several letters have been surgically removed, but I can still make out some of the words: *l—he* (*leche*, milk), *sab—o* (*sabroso*, tasty), *vitam—as* (*vitaminas*, vitamins). The faint odor of sour milk lingers, and a waxy coating gums my fingers. I let go.

As Ethan and I drink the last of our water, the tree flashes shy smiles of faded azure, as if to say, "How do I look? Like my outfit?" The effect falls flat, failing to disguise its bedraggled, trash-covered condition.

We crest a balding hill and I finally see the rancho on the next hilltop. A wispy pencil sketch of a home, it looks as incongruous on that harsh pinnacle as the costumed lemon we met along the way. What an odd place for a house. Today it absorbs the heat and winds of the dry season. I shudder to think of September's relentless rains.

Today's *junta* (workday) is a rite of passage for Ethan and me. Since he first arrived, back in October, no one has thought to include us as a couple in a community workday. A group from the village is gathering today to complete a community dugout canoe. I am giddy with self-importance, a sense of belonging, making a first society appearance with my betrothed.

But as we walk, my mind wades into troubled waters. Even if I'm finally accepted into what passes for Tranquilla society, I still find myself isolated professionally. Román Diego recently dropped by unannounced, and he found me sequestered at home rather than planting corn with the UCLA. He wanted an explanation. I decided to confide in him, feeling conflicted as I spilled the details.

ProTec, an organization with a mission to build small businesses in rural areas of the developing world, has been promoting the use of pesticides and chemical fertilizers for projects sponsored by UCLA. Recently, one of their technicians advised the application of the herbicide Paraquat to control weeds in the plantain field. Two of the younger farmers volunteered to apply it, doing so without proper safety equipment. The cooperative store now sells 2,4-D, so Tranquilla shoppers can purchase the most widely used herbicide in the world when they pick up a pound of rice or a can of tuna.

As I told Román about my concerns, I couldn't shake the feeling of tattling on my neighbors. The community is UCLA, UCLA the community. The people of Tranquilla claw at any shred of promise for a better life. Pesticides seem an easy solution to so many of their concerns that they are blind to the dangers.

"*No puede ser*" (That cannot be). Román was incredulous. "The use of pesticides within the park is strictly prohibited. The regulations could not be clearer."

My thoughts now turn to the young couple I visited just the other day to meet their baby. Beaming, euphoric over the birth of their first child, the father proudly showed me all their preparations, saying, "I even got rid of all the *bichos* [bugs] in the house to make it safe for the *niño* [child]!"

I perked up, eager to know—given the burgeoning bicho problem in my own home—how they had accomplished this feat. "I sprayed an entire container of Malathion," he chuckled. "*Sí, hombre* [Yes, sir], that really did the trick." Malathion has numerous consequences for human health, including permanent lung and kidney damage, even death.

As Ethan and I draw closer to the rancho, I'm still brooding over the pesticides. Román's words come back to me: "Very serious charges. Are you prepared to help me look into this?"

Although I agreed to his plan, it will certainly make life more difficult. He insisted that each of us talk with our supervisors within the next few weeks. The Peace Corps and INRENARE will then use our respective channels to confront ProTec about its promotion of agrochemicals within Chagres National Park. We will convene a joint meeting with ProTec, the Peace Corps, and INRENARE, after which we will decide on the next steps.

Ethan and I arrive at the rancho winded and parched. We find Señor Pablo's wife alone in her rustic kitchen. She acknowledges us with a nod as she works on meal preparations.

"We're here for the *junta*," I chirp, like a child arriving at a playmate's birthday party.

After a few minutes, our hostess introduces herself as Lupe. "Have a seat. You're thirsty?" She offers us *chicha de arroz* (sweetened rice beverage). Locals consider it to be a treat, but we gag on the drink, which is by turns watery and lumpy. Lupe places a soup kettle on the fire stones, splashes corn oil into the pot, and tosses in a few handfuls of rice, which sizzle and darken to a golden brown.

There is no sign of anyone else, so we assume we are the first to arrive. Perched on a wooden bench in the open-air kitchen, we take in the striking barrenness of the immediate landscape. The house rattles as the midday breeze picks up, and I find myself thinking of the lemon tree, surely a whirl of blue by now.

After a few minutes, we have drunk a polite amount of the chicha. I ask when she might be expecting Pablo. She stares at us blankly and then points to a path leading down the hill. "Oh, in a few hours I guess. *La gente* [the people] have been working all morning, *allá arriba* [way up there]."

Crap! Our big debut, and we've almost missed it. We stammer our excuses and set out to find the others.

The dense, brushy growth of the forest contrasts with the hardscrabble surroundings of Pablo's hut. We set out tentatively along the tangled, indistinct path and listen for the salamando. When we finally hear the distinctly Panamanian yodels, they sound weary, downtrodden. We plunge into the woods and bushwhack toward the sounds of the work party.

As the workers come into view, the irony of today's task confronts me. I am a Peace Corps forester charged with stemming the tide of deforestation in the Panama Canal watershed. Today, however, we will help a group of campesinos exploit one of the few remaining supracanopy trees in the area. The junta we proudly join undermines the conservation mission I serve. I am officially part of the problem.

The challenge before us is simple in concept: moving the vessel from land to water. It is a single step in the long process of making a large dugout canoe. A few months ago, several men felled a huge *espavé* (wild cashew, *Anacardium excelsum*) tree with axes, dangerous work. They returned with hatchets, machetes, and planers to carve and sculpt it into a crude but recognizable cayuco. The final step will be to further smooth and hone the boat once it's on the lakeshore. But first we have to get it there.

The men barely notice us. A few of them grunt, perhaps in greeting, perhaps not. They keep working as Ethan slides in seamlessly. I watch to pick up on the rhythm. The men in front provide a three-two-one countdown, and everyone heaves in unison as they progress a few feet. The work is painfully slow as they repeat this sequence again and again in the oppressive heat. I hesitate to join, unable to banish the notion that these men are pallbearers, the canoe a massive corpse.

I try in vain to resummon the enthusiasm that brought us here earlier this morning. "After all," I tell myself, "there is no question the community needs a new dugout." Indeed, the old one has sprung several irreparable leaks, such that someone is always dedicated exclusively to bailing when they use it. For supply runs, emergencies, and visiting other communities, group transportation is a must. The new boat will seat twenty-four and last ten years. I press my way into the huddle.

A two-man crew swings machetes to part the forest before us. Even so, branches lash our faces, necks, and arms. A small stump catches the toe of one of my boots, and it flaps uselessly from the sole. I am dismayed by the heft of our load—it must weigh a ton. Thirst settles into my bones, and I grow dizzy. The odor of fermenting wood exacerbates my wooziness.

Grit mingles with the boat's grain, rubbing my fingers raw. I have had enough. I drop out, defeated. The group disappears down the hill as I sit with legs bent to rest my head on my knees. I realize I have no idea how to get back to the house.

I stand up shakily and stumble through the undergrowth, searching for a trail or anything at all familiar. Thrashing about for a while, I pause to catch my breath and reorient myself. I pant as I peer first in front of me and then behind. When I tilt my head to the side I glimpse a snatch of blue, and then another. The lemon tree! If it could speak, it would tease me a little: "The path has been here all along, you know." As I ascend the hill, a sense of failure mingles with the great relief of recognizing my whereabouts.

Arriving at the rancho a few minutes later, I collapse on the bench. "That sure was hard work."

Lupe stares, unsympathetic, harried. She bangs a few pots and hurls a glob of tomato paste into the stew to lessen its pallor. She sweeps the packed dirt floor with more zeal than necessary.

"That was no job for a woman," she scolds. "And me, here, with all this food to prepare. Why do you think I asked you here? I needed help in the kitchen." She flounces onto a chair, making a show of flapping a fan of woven palm under her chin.

I blush under her admonishment. A few awkward minutes pass and I try to busy myself before the first of the workers arrives. I grab a stack of shallow enameled bowls and set them near the kettle. As the men straggle in, they assemble on benches, spent from their efforts. I copy Lupe as she serves the stew. No one mentions my transgression further, but the mood is somber and silent apart from the sound of slurping.

Finally, Ethan arrives with the last bunch. His clothes are filthy and torn, and he has several scrapes and bruises. But the men all joke and slap him on the back. He is embraced by their circle of masculinity while I fume on the sidelines. I relocated to rural Panamá to conserve forests, not to make lunch. But Tranquilla has its own ideas about women's work.

We head home after the meal, stopping to admire the boat, which rests on the shore. It is a beauty. We launch our own, smaller cayuco. Two gringos on the waters of Lake Alajuela, we would not stand out much more if we dressed ourselves in dozens of blue milk cartons. Oh, we may learn Spanish, paddle around in a dugout canoe, and wear sombreros, but, like the lemon tree, we are merely in costume. And Lupe knows it.

10

Todo el Mundo

The school year ends, but I have permission to use the classroom. Before the teacher left town, we discussed a summer project: painting a map of the world right on the wall. She gave me a key to the school, and Ethan and I have been making plans.

Using instructions from a Peace Corps publication, we first create a grid on the wall and then pencil in the country boundaries. The exercise is complicated by the recent breakup of the Soviet Union. Ethan improvises the separation of the newly fractured republics and sketches them in. It takes several tries to get Eastern Europe right, but once satisfied with the outline, we trace over all the borders with a permanent marker.

Now we need painting supplies. We have odds and ends of leftover paint from projects at the school and church. Ethan brings a new Sharpie he begged off a Smithsonian researcher last week. We'll use that to better define the boundaries once the paint dries.

But we need a few more colors and assorted sizes of paintbrushes. This calls for a trip into the city. It's just as well, because we have one more thing to finish up before we can get our marriage license—an AIDS test. But that will be achieved easily compared to the barrier we faced a few weeks before, when Ethan was almost deported.

As we were applying for our marriage license, standing in line after line and finding more obstacles than answers, one official finally informed us that Ethan could not marry anybody in Panamá unless he had a work permit. He could not get a work permit unless he had the appropriate visa. Upon scrutinizing Ethan's visa, the same official decreed that it was not valid.

"I have no idea who approved this, but I assure you there is no such thing as a one-year tourist visa in Panamá. The longest stay we grant our tourists is three months. So your visa has expired as far as I am concerned. Next!"

Crushed, we walked back over to the Peace Corps office on Via España. I stopped at the bathroom to splash cold water on my tear-streaked face. My eyes were still red and puffy, but I looked a little more presentable.

Justin found us sitting on the couch in the Volunteer lounge, Ethan with his arm around me. "Hey. Ethan passed his background check." The Peace Corps had to do a security check to make sure Ethan didn't have a felony record, I suppose. He came up clean. "So, uh, why the long faces?"

We told him we were getting nowhere with the license, and that Ethan might in fact have to leave Panamá in the near future. Justin remembered the attorney who worked down the hall from the Peace Corps office. "This guy seems to love us. He's stopped by and told me more than once that if he can help us in any way, to be sure to let him know. Even better, his specialty is immigration."

Justin walked us down to the attorney's office and introduced us. The attorney was very friendly and saw us right away. He asked a few questions before saying, "There are a number of things we could try. But I think the simplest would be for me to call Panamá's subdirector of immigration. He'll know how to help us."

The attorney, whom I now thought of as "our" attorney, picked up the phone and connected immediately with the subdirector. He switched to Spanish and told him our story. He ended the call with "Right. Good. They should be down there within half an hour." It was three o'clock. He hung up and said to us, "I should think you could make it there in half an hour. The subdirector is expecting you. He's having a letter prepared. With his signature and seal things should go smoothly for you." We thanked him profusely and shook hands. "It is a pleasure to help the Peace Corps."

"Kinda offended my record came up squeaky clean," Ethan joked as we walked back to Immigration. We both liked to think of ourselves as mavericks, outside the mainstream. Regardless of how hard we tried, the two of us were incorrigible in our wholesomeness, no matter how many Gulf War protests we may have marched in. It felt good to laugh, though, and it was definitely a relief that Ethan had cleared yet another hurdle.

With the subdirector's letter in hand, and a new one-year special permit that allowed Ethan to volunteer or do paid work, we sailed right through the same lines that had stultified us earlier in the day. The last official eyed us suspiciously, as if to say, "I know you're up to no good here, but there's really not much I can do about it." You'd think someone might have offered a kind word of congratulations. "Oh, you're getting married? How nice. Many happy returns." But they were all business all the time at the Immigration Office.

The AIDS test is easy in comparison. At least we need not involve any lawyers. This is not something the Peace Corps nurse is authorized to do for me, so we pay for the test out of pocket. We simply get off our bus, walk to a clinic, and a nurse draws our blood. Shortly after his sample is drawn, Ethan goes white, says he feels light-headed, and lies down. The nurse is concerned, but he explains, "This always happens to me when I give blood."

"Plus, we've been under a lot of stress," I offer.

He's better by the time the nurse returns with certificates that attest to a clean bill of health. We head over to the Machetazo, a huge department store, and buy the paints and brushes before heading to the bus terminal. There we part ways. Ethan is off to his job at the Smithsonian Tropical Research Institute and I head home.

A few days later, back in Tranquilla, I round up three kids to help paint the world map that Ethan and I started on the wall. They are full of questions.

"Which one is Panamá?" they demand to know. Then, gasping, "So tiny?"

"Show us *los Estados Unidos* [the United States]!" they insist. "Much bigger!"

I assign each child a country to paint. Each dips a brush into one of the many jars of colored paint, which they apply with a surprising amount of care and patience. The children are proudly at work when a stranger walks in. "They told me I would find you here." He smiles and shakes my hand. "Esteban Gonzalez, at your service." He has a mustache and wears a baseball hat. Despite the intense heat, he looks neat and cool, dressed for the field.

As the kids paint, Esteban and I fall into easy conversation, and I learn he is a new technician with the Ministry of Agriculture. I tell him about my projects and he listens attentively. He is enthusiastic when I describe my philosophy of starting small and making slow, gradual progress. He asks if I would be available the next day to show him around.

I am smitten with Esteban's interest in my work, to say nothing of the respect he showed in approaching me directly to learn about it. "Wow," I think. "This guy might be different from the other technicians."

"Sure. What time can you get in from the city?" He surprises me by announcing his intention to spend the night *aquí mismo* (right here) in Tranquilla.

"I can be ready at any time." This is unheard of. Government workers are notorious for watching the clock. They certainly never spend the night in the villages they serve.

Initially eager to work with other organizations, I became frustrated with the usual alphabet soup of development workers and government extension agents I encountered early in my Peace Corps service. ProTec and its flagrant disregard for the park's laws and regulations represent an extreme. The others strike me at best as an uncoordinated, useless bunch.

Fortunately, many organizations pose a mere annoyance in their ineffectiveness and unreliability. Those that build enthusiasm and then fail to follow through, however, actually undermine my work. They erode the already low morale of rural farmers, who then become even less likely to experiment with new techniques. As a result, I have learned to be skeptical, even suspicious, of others who say they want to work in this community or elsewhere in the park.

In contrast, Esteban seems to espouse the go-slow approach, to develop a real understanding for the community before leaping into a project. He actually says one day, "Give a man a fish, and he will have fish for supper. Teach a man to fish, and he will eat for a lifetime." He has me hook, line, and sinker.

As promised, the following day we visit two of my project sites. The first is a neighbor's distant finca, where we have planted on a contour to control soil erosion. Using principally *balo* (quick stick, *Gliricidia sepium*), a soil-enriching tree commonly used as live stakes for "living fences," we have stabilized the slope in anticipation of planting crops. The other is Señor Pablo's place. I must check his orange seedlings, and he has a new vegetable garden on a steep hillside.

Neither of the two farmers is home, as these are surprise visits. Still, they give Esteban a picture of what we are working with. Both are very long walks and we have neither food nor water. At the end of the day, we call it quits. I am anxious to return home and cook a meal in anticipation of Ethan's return from his job at the research institute. Esteban wants to get home to his family in the city. He says he will return over the weekend, with his wife and children.

"Right," I think. The cynical part of me is sure that great though he seems, this is the last Tranquilla will see of Esteban Gonzalez. I have learned never to trust anything that a technician from *afuera* (outside) says.

To my utter astonishment, who should emerge from a hired cayuco on Saturday morning but the entire Gonzalez family, complete with wife, two children, and a dog. They fish all day and then cook up a huge stew in the church kitchen, where they are camped. They invite the whole village to stop by.

"Bring your own bowls and spoons," they shout. "We don't have anything with us but these clothes we are wearing!"

This guy has the skill of a politician. But he is an agronomist. Is it really possible that he is different?

Before they leave on Sunday, Esteban tells me he will return the following week to meet with the farmers whose projects we visited the week prior.

"Can you set it up with them, so they, you know, expect us?"

On Monday, I hike to Señor Pablo's place, nervous that I might not find him at home, and also nervous that I might. If no one is home, my only option is to wait for their return at a respectful distance from the house. Leaving a note is iffy given Tranquilla's high rate of illiteracy.

I have not seen Pablo and Lupe since the junta incident. Lupe is home after all, and I am relieved to find her civil, if not warm. It is just before lunchtime, so we wait for her husband's certain return. When Pablo appears, he seems pleased that a technician wants to visit. He wants to show off the new garden.

"Maybe we can take a look at those oranges, too," I pipe in, perhaps too eagerly. The oranges are a sore spot with me, as they need grafting and have been in limbo for months. Señor Pablo keeps canceling on me.

"*Sí, cómo no*" (Sure, why not).

My neighbor's distant field is another matter. The man, aged beyond his fifty-some-odd years, lives in town, just two huts up from mine. I can ask him anytime, which I do the next day. He is willing but unenthusiastic.

Slurring through his remaining teeth, he manages, "Oh, I have been thinking of giving up that finca. It is very far away. I am old. But all right." This response pains me, because much of our work will pay off only in the long term. I would hate to see him give it up now.

True to his word again, Esteban comes to visit the following week. We first hike to Señor Pablo's. Examining his hillside vegetable garden, we can barely contain our frustration. He has followed my advice to plant in rows but has positioned them vertically, up and down the hill rather than horizontally, parallel to the contours.

"That way, the water can run straight, straight, straight down the slope," he says proudly. He gestures and whistles through his teeth as if to indicate just how rapidly the water will drain.

Yeah, and take all your topsoil with it, I fume darkly, still holding my tongue.

Esteban, on the other hand, dishes out a surprising amount of criticism. For all their shortcomings, most technicians are at least nonconfrontational, but in this setting he lashes out at Pablo for his approach and the loss of his soil. I am taken aback and to some extent find myself taking Pablo's side, despite my disagreement with his practices.

More disappointing yet, my elderly neighbor is not home when we stop by. Gonzalez says he will come back Friday. Later, when I see my neighbor, I berate the poor man, telling him that he embarrassed me in front of my Panamanian colleague, made it look like he didn't care about his project. Haggard and slight in his advanced years, he is perhaps the most defenseless of all the potential victims of my self-righteousness. I feel ashamed.

The following Friday, I decide to do laundry while I wait for Esteban. As I stand at the spigot with my tub of soapy work clothes, I take out my frustrations by scrubbing extra hard with the brush. At least I can get something done instead of waiting around.

As I work, what started out as a dull ache in my left lower back becomes more painful. I hang the laundry on the hibiscus hedge and climb into bed exhausted. Esteban never shows.

Ethan is away all day. When he returns, I am asleep and the house is dark. He makes some pasta and wakes me, but I feel too nauseated to eat. He props me up on the bench beside him and I vomit. The following morning, I take aspirin and Ethan massages my back with Bengay several times. I start to suspect I have something more than a backache and read through the Peace Corps medical manual, *Donde no hay doctor* (*Where There Is No Doctor*).

I conclude that I have a kidney infection. I have some sulfa drugs in the medical kit and take a dose. The next day I take another, and after a few more days in bed I feel well again. I have enough pills to last until my next trip into Panama City, when I'll get the Peace Corps nurse to check me out.

Esteban does not return during my week of sickness, which is probably to the good. When he finally does come to Tranquilla, my cynicism is once again entrenched. Nonetheless, we find my neighbor at home and we hike to his finca. I bring along our crude equipment, a *nivel en A* (A-frame level), which we used originally to delineate the contours of the hillside plot. It consists of three young saplings lashed together to form a capital letter *A*. From the peak of the *A* hangs a rock on a string. When the A-frame is positioned on the level, the rock hangs straight down in the center of it.

We demonstrate its use along a complete row and describe our plans for planting pineapple and hillside rice.

"No, no, no, no, no," says Esteban. "We are going to do something *pero grande* [much bigger]!" He paints a verbal picture of an expansive, lush garden bursting forth with a cornucopia of mixed fruits and vegetables. In short, he insults the project we have been working on until now and promises my neighbor the world.

I sadly size up my former ally. In mere weeks, he has scared off two of my clients—one by telling the farmer he was doing it all wrong, and the other by telling him he wasn't dreaming nearly big enough. Things are awkward between Pablo and me after this. We never finish the orange project and do not start any new projects together. Although I continue to be friendly with my neighbor, he loses interest altogether in his hillside finca.

I decide to try thinking of Esteban as a professional mirage. He represents for me the stimulating professional links that I craved, especially at the beginning of my service. Fortunately, as my community ties strengthen, the external ties decline in importance, at least emotionally. From here on out I work in and for Tranquilla alone. What felt like isolation months ago now feels more like professional independence.

A few weeks later, I work with a few more kids to paint the finishing touches on the world map's bright blue oceans before the teacher returns and the new school year begins. *Pacífico* (Pacific) reads one label, *Atlántico* (Atlantic) another, and so on. I resolve to be not the one who promises the world, but the one who paints it on the wall for all to see.

11

Acacia

The chiva drops us off at Corotú after a week of training with fellow Volunteers in Panama City. Ethan and I are both exhausted from the long, dusty return trip to Lake Alajuela. We rummage through the vegetation for our canoe paddles. Like bikes in Amsterdam, all manner of cayucos clutter the outskirts of Corotú. The boats are fastened with padlocks to the larger trees, but paddles are more difficult to secure. We hide them in the underbrush following the local custom. We part the grass carefully—it serves the additional function of public privy. The undergrowth reeks of stale urine and piles of human excrement lurk about.

Our boat seems a little less seaworthy than we remember. A few weeks ago, some of the cracks on the hull widened, and the leaking worsened. Ethan sculpted a wide plank that now sits in the boat and serves two purposes: to keep the bum of the bow-sitter dry, and to distribute more weight toward the sides rather than the bottom. It works pretty well, but the lake is choppy today. My faith in our trusty vessel wanes.

We tentatively launch our tired, thirsty selves into Lake Alajuela. Looking up, we suddenly see the impossible hurtling toward us in the form of a powerboat towing a blonde water-skier. A flash of bright yellow, our intruder sports sunglasses and, yes, a bikini. I have already made the mental shift toward conservative dress upon entering the campo (countryside) after our trip to the city, and quick disapproval skitters through my mind: *Well, I never!*

We point the nose of our cayuco into the powerboat's waves to avoid capsizing, and we mull over this improbable occurrence. A jousting match between armored knights would have seemed no stranger than this spectacle.

The powerboat disappears for a few minutes. It seems it has gone partway up the Chagres River. We paddle hard to put as much distance as possible between us and its likely trajectory. Our guess is a good one, and when the boat returns the turbulence subsides by the time it reaches us. The blonde waves.

As we near Tranquilla, Ethan points out a Sunfish sailboat in the distance. We are equally perplexed by this quieter display, given the usual earthiness of Lake Alajuela watercraft, hewn from local materials. Even the roomier motorboats are dugout canoes; the motors put-put-put at a slow speed that is at best a trot, allowing fumes to gather around the passengers. We stare but cannot get a good look at the sailor. Who are these people? Are there gringos in our midst?

We ask around.

"Oh, that's just the *Ingeniero* [Engineer]," we are told. "He spends his weekends here at his finca. He is very rich. A *Rabiblanco*." We've heard about Rabiblancos but have never met one in person. Rabiblancos, literally "white tails," are Panamanians of nearly pure Spanish descent, in contrast to the predominant mestizos of mixed cultural backgrounds.

The following weekend, the fancy motorboat approaches Tranquilla's main muelle. A handsome campesino, dapper in a new sombrero, disembarks. He asks for the gringos and finds his way to our rancho. Saturday mugs of coffee in hand, we read the note he hands us. It is written in perfect English:

Dear Peace Corps,
    Won't you join us for some lunch? Mateo will bring you over for a cookout.
    —José Navarro and family

Ethan and I are not by nature spontaneous people. Today, though, we look at each other and shrug. Why not? The laundry is drying in the sun, our breakfast dishes are already washed, and we have no plans. An otherwise dreary weekend sprawls before us.

We climb gingerly into the spotless boat under the stares of the handful of villagers gathered at the store. We are self-conscious of our muddy shoes and the possibility of dirtying the vessel, a brilliant white in the midmorning sun. Who will we find on the other side?

On a shore of the lake we have never seen before, Navarro stands expectantly on his manmade beach. Tall and elegant, he is dressed in a *guayabera* (a multi-pocket sport shirt popular throughout Central and South America and the Caribbean), khaki shorts, and flip-flops. Holding a bottle of Coke, he opens his arms wide to welcome us. We shake hands and he tells us to call him José.

José also introduces us to his wife and son and offers us soft drinks. A teenager pads into the picnic area wearing a white cover-up and toweling off her hair. The blonde. She smiles broadly as he introduces her as his daughter. We later find out that José is his middle name, and that everyone else calls him Eduardo. They find it funny that we call him José but gradually come to accept it.

"Ah, the Peace Corps," he says wistfully. He pronounces it "corpse," and we don't correct him. "I tell my children you are like a modern nun." We learn that the entire Navarro family loves gringos, just for being gringos. We get the sense we are something of a status symbol at their party. They show us off to their friends.

We jump at every chance to visit them. For a few hours at a time, we step out of our squalor, roar away in the gleaming boat, and have a picnic at the lake house, much as we would in America. Munching hot dogs and potato chips, slurping soda, and chatting about our lives in America are central to these gatherings. Each visit is made a little more delicious by a sense of infidelity, both to Tranquilla and to what is essentially a two-year oath of poverty and the Peace Corps Way of Life. In many ways, Navarro and his family become our *patrónes* (benefactors). After each party, they send us home with Oreos, Doritos, and other assorted junk food, the packaging obscenely colorful in our shabby home.

"*Qué rico* [how sweet]," says Navarro's wife, upon seeing our rancho early in our budding friendship. They are charmed.

Upon learning of my focus on forestry, Navarro shows us around his finca. We admire the many fruit trees and his straight, healthy rows of teak. He is eager to experiment and shows us his eucalypts. "Only seven years old," he tells us. "Just look at them!"

Indeed, their stately forms tower on the lakeshore. They stand as noble sentinels guarding the finca from harsh winds that roll off the lake.

"But you know what I really want?" He asks us one day.

We don't.

"I already have eucalypts. Now I need acacia [black wattle, *Acacia mangium*]. Soon, I will be Finca Australia!" He tells us of a friend who planted acres of the nitrogen-fixing tree. "It's *that* fast growing. Plant this tree and the soil will be rich for years to come." Well. We are interested.

On our next visit, José presents us with a large envelope full of tiny black enameled seeds. The acacia. "Find someone to grow these for me. I will pay him twenty-five cents per tree." My heart soars. Suddenly, I have my first small-income-generating project. I return to Tranquilla, gleeful in the certainty that the first family I offer this project to will jump at the chance. Not only is it a chance to earn a little sorely needed cash, but it will also boost trees in the esteem of local residents.

"*Sí, cómo no*," is the lackadaisical response from the first few would-be nurserymen. In other words, "Whatever."

"*Mucho trabajo* [a lot of work]," says another disappointingly unenterprising young man.

Then, I think of the industrious Señor Lorenzo. He remains one of my favorite neighbors, although I am not sure it is mutual. Perhaps I think of him as a father figure given that he and his family fed me during my first few months in Tranquilla. He also helped me on several around-the-house projects before Ethan arrived.

I cannot think of the compact, sturdy Señor Lorenzo without also thinking of his bedraggled sombrero. I have never seen him without it, nor without his scraggly beard. Rather than going barefoot as do many of his compadres, Señor Lorenzo wears *cutarras* (sandals) he makes from old tires. As creative as he is enterprising, Señor Lorenzo practices many of the traditional arts. He weaves hats and bags, carves wood, and plays accordion in the local *típico* (folk band). He is also always short on cash.

When I bring up the topic of growing acacia, he replies, to my chagrin, "*Cómo no*." Disgusted, I half decide to grow the damned trees myself.

The following day, however, Señor Lorenzo appears again. "So, I made the semillero," he announces. "When do we start?"

"Right this instant," is my unhesitating reply. I mentally slap my forehead. Time after time, I resolve to play hard to get, but in my desperation I seldom remember to project this demeanor.

We scrounge fertile soil for filling the nursery bags. This time, I manage to steer clear of the water main. In all, there is room for six hundred individual bags in the semillero, a respectable start. We salivate over the potential income, which could be as much as $150 in pure profit, more than many campesinos make in a year.

In each filled bag we sow five of the glistening seeds. Watering them, I get a snug feeling as I imagine them settling in. Germination can be explosive in the tropics, where natural processes operate on fast-forward. From decomposition to lush growth, the pace has left me breathless more than once. As I admire the tidy rows of plump little bags, my hopes are high.

I contain myself for a few days and then sprint over to Lorenzo's rancho to inspect progress. No germination yet, not totally unexpected. We wait.

A week later, we are still waiting.

And the following week, we are still waiting.

Fortunately, Ethan and I now have the plans for our wedding in a few days to distract us. "Plans" actually overstates things. Some would describe what we are about to embark on as an elopement. But we don't see it that way, and we're certainly not trying to escape anything or anyone. In fact, we are headed to the airport to pick up my mother and her husband, Todd, who will attend our civil ceremony in a few days.

Once they arrive, we check them into a room at the Hotel California, which is on Via España but on a less posh stretch than the Peace Corps office. The hotel will be our base for several days while we have family in Panamá. I make a quick outing to Avenida Central, where I buy a seven-dollar wedding "gown," a sundress in aqua blue with a black paisley pattern. All our Peace Corps friends arrive from their communities, and we go out on the town for our respective bachelor and bachelorette parties. Suffice it to say that what goes on at these parties does not bear repeating. Although I fare better overall than Ethan, we both have horrible hangovers the morning after. Our wedding day.

Todd drives us in the rental car to the Peace Corps office to pick up Chloe, my very best Peace Corps friend. She agreed some months ago to be one of our two required witnesses—Todd will be the other since it has to be someone unrelated by blood to either bride or groom. "You remembered your passport, right? For identification?" I ask Chloe as we get into the car.

"Shit! Shit, shit, shit!"

"God, Chloe! I'll take that as a no! I think we have enough time to get back to the hotel and grab it before we head to the courthouse."

"No! I mean, forgot it, like in my site! It's in Santa Rita!"

All five of us are in a panic as Todd does a full U-turn and starts heading back toward the Hotel Ideál, where the other Volunteers are staying. Surely someone has a passport with them?

"You have got to be kidding!" Ethan curses in frustration as a police car turns on its siren and pulls us over. Apparently that U-turn was not such a good idea. Ethan and I negotiate with the police officer, and things look bad. It appears that we are going to have to go in to headquarters and spend the rest of the day filling out forms of various kinds.

"But it's our wedding day! We're trying to get to the courthouse for our ceremony! It's in a little over an hour!"

The officer is unmoved. He looks away for a few seconds and then looks back at us expectantly. He cannot exactly ask us for money, but he discreetly makes the sign for cash, rubbing his fingers together. Finally, I understand. One of our diplomat friends once told me in passing that bribery is the unspoken, yet most common, way of settling traffic violations in Panamá. I never thought I would have to deal with it since Peace Corps Volunteers are not allowed to drive. But deal with it now I must.

"Todd. Please bribe this officer of the law."

"But it's clear he . . ."

"For God's sake, Todd," my mother cuts him off. "This is not the time to show off your moral fiber!"

Todd hands over twenty dollars. The cop is unimpressed. Another bill is passed through the window, and he tilts his head a little as if to ask, "Really? You think this will get you off the hook?"

"Here! This is all I have. If it's not enough that's just too bad." Todd empties his wallet. Here it is $120 later, and the cop finally waves us on.

We clip along, with about fifty minutes to go before our appointment. But in a few minutes a huge traffic jam snags us. Although we are only six blocks from the Hotel Ideál, it seems unlikely we will get there. Chloe tells me some of the room numbers where I might find the other Volunteers and wishes me luck. The others will wait for me in the car on the corner of the road that will take us downtown, about five minutes from the courthouse.

I set off running and don't stop until I get to the first room number Chloe has given me—252. I knock on the door to find my friend Karen squinting into the hallway. "But aren't you and Chloe supposed to be . . ."

"Yes! Chloe forgot her passport! Did you happen to bring yours?"

"Sorry, man. Didn't think I'd need it. Try Catherine's room. She's two doors down."

Catherine is just as bleary eyed, but good-naturedly gets dressed, grabs her passport, and dashes with me out of the Ideál and through the crowded

Avenida Central. We make it to the courthouse just in time. Ironically, the judge is delayed, and we end up waiting nearly an hour later than scheduled for the no-frills ceremony in Spanish. A tailgate party ensues among our little group, including a champagne toast in the courthouse parking lot.

Shortly after, we meet our friends for a picnic lunch with cake and champagne in a nearby park. Chloe apologizes again for forgetting her passport and then plays Beatles love songs on her flute. I clutch an armful of white roses and baby's breath and am alarmed to find the dye from my wedding dress has cast a green hue upon my skin. Ethan kisses my cheek and says, "We did it, didn't we?" then does a handstand. Hugs and sandwiches, toothpaste-sweet frosting, and more toasts. We realize we have no plan for the leftover cake, so we give it to a group of Boy Scouts in the next picnic shelter. They cannot believe their luck.

My mother and Todd want to see Tranquilla for themselves. We return there the next day, visitors in tow. The first thing I do is drop by Lorenzo's house to check the acacia seeds. We see our first glimmer of life. In a few of the pots, the faintest sketches of seedlings have unfurled. A sparse constellation of green has begun to creep across the microlandscape of the semillero. Hardly an impressive start, but hope remains.

Right after taking my mother and Todd back to the airport for their flight home, I succumb to a fit of mistimed practicality. I stop by the Peace Corps office to research the requirements for growing acacia. I am mortified to learn that we have skipped an important step, a common technique for propagating tropical trees. A hot-water bath can improve germination rates tenfold, not to mention shorten the time between sowing and sprouting. What should have been a sure thing for Lorenzo and his family is suddenly much more tentative. Do I tell him?

Fortunately, the oversight leads to mere disappointment, not disaster. With careful redistribution of seedlings that have sprouted a few to a bag, we consolidate our successful hatchlings into one corner of the semillero. Watering becomes easier and the seedlings thrive. By September, we have around 150 seedlings four to six inches tall. The majority have developed the characteristic broad, flattened stem of a maturing seedling that is ready to plant. A far cry from the 600 we hoped for, but still, it's something.

The day comes when we load them into motetes and fill Lorenzo's boat. We ferry them to José Navarro, who greets us as usual with outstretched arms. We unload the boat, and José praises the seedlings, sturdy and full of promise. The daily wage for one campesino doing hard labor in the fields is five dollars. Today, Lorenzo pockets forty dollars in cash, possibly the easiest money he has ever earned.

Our transaction complete, we thank Navarro and shake hands. As we leave shore, Señor Lorenzo thanks me. "*Le agradesco a ustéd también*" (I am grateful to you, too).

I tell him it is my pleasure; I enjoyed working on the project. "I could not have done this alone," I say. "It was really your family's hard work that made it happen." I suggest that next time we'll do the right seed treatment, and we can grow even more.

"*Cómo no.*"

12

Hormigas

"Get up!" Ethan hisses. He shakes me. "Get out of bed!"

Sleep clings to me in the blurred darkness of the rancho. Ethan shakes me again. He yelps and aims a flashlight at his foot. A fearsome ant grips his instep and he flings the creature aside. A swarm of ants surges by the outskirts of Ethan's flashlight beam, still pointed at the foot of the bed. We are under attack.

Ethan scrambles over me, lights the kerosene lamp, and drags me off the bed. We huddle on an island of earthen floor as living rivulets stream around us. Ants flow in sheets across the mattress.

True to their name, army ants loot and ransack as they march across tropical landscapes. Academic accounts of nomadic ants fascinated me long before my first forestry job brought me to this rural village in post-Noriega Panamá. In practice, however, I find the assault repulsive.

Army ants are equal-opportunity raiders of village and jungle alike. Our traditional rancho of sticks and bark is one of a cluster of equally organic dwellings ringed by scrub. From the ants' perspective our home is just another place to search for prey.

We escape to the kitchen, where we try to move the troops along. Smashing a few here and there provides a brief, if false, sense of empowerment. We soon resort to heavier artillery. I spray a concentrated repellent along a formation as it snakes across a shelf. This intervention stuns the ants momentarily, but they simply shift their column a few inches and persevere.

Our next strategy is even more desperate. Selecting the densest throng, we douse the dirt floor with kerosene and drop a match. A gratifying sizzle ensues as the blaze chars dozens of little bodies, but we quickly abandon this tactic. We live, after all, in a structure made of kindling.

Our counterattacks cause only slight confusion among the ranks. Corpse removal thwarts progress, prolongs the siege. We relax a little as we emerge from our sleep-fog and remember how these insects operate. They will move on, with or without us. Our best option is to wait them out, leave them to their plunder.

We retreat to a bench and watch. Each individual fills a role; none is entirely self-sufficient. Warriors defend the colony, menacing pincers ready for action. Nannies cradle larvae, functioning as mobile nurseries. Laborers shoulder the spoils gathered on the journey. Managers use their bossy pheromones to keep the others in line. The intruders carry off all manner of vermin: grubs, cockroaches, spiders. We had no idea the palm thatching of our roof harbored such horror.

Still drowsy, my house occupied by a foreign army, I imagine that night in 1989 when US marines invaded Panama City to oust General Manuel Noriega. Operation Just Cause.

I slap each cheek. Did I really just liken the insects in my kitchen to the US invasion of Panamá? As if our present circumstances bear any resemblance to a military action with thousands of casualties, tens of thousands rendered homeless in the bombing.

Activity subsides in the kitchen after a couple of hours, and we peer into the bedroom. The last of the glossy hordes recedes, coursing from chair to desktop, wall post to ceiling. They pour through a few crevices and disappear.

Sunrise finds us dazed, sleep deprived. Reaching for my shoe, I find a loathsome backwater of soldiers circling angrily inside it. I toss the stragglers into the yard. They have lost direction and will perish without their colony. I can only hope Ethan and I, two gringos isolated from friends and family in the United States, will fare better.

A neighbor shuffles by.

"*Hormigas* [ants]?" he asks. We nod. He grins.

"Thought so. I saw your light on last night. They can be *muy bravo* [very fierce], *no*?" We nod again, tongue-tied, as he walks on.

For weeks following the incursion, we marvel at the cleanliness of our rooms. I feel something akin to gratitude. As the ants spirited away our household pests, they also swept us into the orbit of community life. News spreads that the gringos survived another rite of passage; our own invader status in the village softens into something more benign.

Was the US invasion benign? Certainly the residents of Panama City suffered far more than a few ant bites, but the nation was cleansed of a brutal dictator. In these parts, my neighbors assure me their daily experience is unchanged by the vagaries of political power at the top. Likewise, legions of ants still wander the jungle. When they come to clean house everyone hunkers down and waits for them to pass.

13

Palmas

Although our palm-constructed house could not forestall an ant invasion, it keeps us relatively dry, shields us to some extent from prying eyes, and shelters our hearts. The diverse family of palms scrawls its signature across daily life in the tropics. Palms meet needs related to housing, hats, basketry, food, and religion, to name a few. The classic image of a coconut palm is tantamount to "tropical paradise."

I make a day trip into Panama City to check in with Justin about the ProTec pesticide issue and pick up a few supplies. If there is time, I will stop by the INRENARE office to see whether Román Diego has made any headway with ProTec.

A mission like today's could totally bomb. Will I be trapped in a purgatory of missed connections? Will Justin be in the office, at a meeting, on vacation, or visiting another Volunteer? Leaving the village is always a leap of faith. But today I'm in luck. Transportation functions seamlessly.

The contrast between the air-conditioned Peace Corps office and the sauna outside perks me up and I make my way to Justin's door. Ecstatic to find him in, I wait outside as he finishes a phone call. A few minutes later, he waves me in and we chat for a while, exchanging pleasantries. He asks what brings me to the big city.

I recount for him the ProTec story and am gratified at his indignation. He finds the situation offensive. ProTec supposedly dedicates itself to sustainability and appropriate technology. In what way is introducing banned chemicals into the protected watershed of Chagres National Park consistent with that mission? I tell him about Román's suggestion that both the Peace Corps and INRENARE contact ProTec.

For my boss, the direction is clear: write to the head of ProTec's Latin

America Program. I craft a pointed letter, the sort that only a self-righteous twenty-two-year-old can muster. The letter documents in detail my observations about ProTec's promotion of chemicals. But do I stop there? No. Instead I segue into listing all my other grievances with the organization's technicians: they are disrespectful; they fail to coordinate workdays with other community events; they fail to show up when they say they will. Justin mails the letter with only a few minor grammatical corrections. He tells me he will be in touch with Román and will also meet with ProTec in the upcoming week. I should return to the city next month.

There's plenty of time left for me to stop by INRENARE before returning to Tranquilla, so Justin phones Román to let him know I'll be stopping by. When I arrive, Román waits outside the headquarters entrance smoking a cigarette. He has a slightly rumpled look about him, but that's not unusual. A five o'clock shadow adorns his face, and he is dressed as usual in faded jeans and running shoes, a polo shirt drooping over his waistline. This is the first time I have seen the man smoke, but it confirms my earlier suspicions. The smell of tobacco always lingers around him, and his complexion is sallow from a habit of many years. His forty-something hand today is missing its wedding band. There is so much to the lives of my Panamanian counterparts that I know nothing about.

He still hasn't been in touch with Augustino Pimentél, the head of ProTec Panamá. "I have been . . . preoccupied" is his only explanation. As I read parts of the ProTec letter to him—translated into Spanish as best I can—he stubs out his cigarette and lights another. Justin and I have forced the issue.

"Has this letter already been mailed?"

I nod.

"Why did you and Justin go around the head of ProTec Panama? Augustino Pimentél is a prideful man. He's not going to like that." Román Diego's tone is businesslike and calm, but his eyes are weary. I don't have an answer for this and say as much. I want to say, "It was Justin's idea. I just went along with it." But somehow I don't think that will win me any points with Román. Román says he'll try to smooth what are sure to be Pimentél's ruffled feathers, if such a thing is possible, in the next few weeks. He'll talk with Justin about what to do from there. God, what a mess.

Román seems to want to end on a positive note and makes small talk about how my trip into the city went today, how my health has been lately; he also inquires about Ethan. He presents an interesting idea for a new project. Many of Panamá's native palms are in decline. If anyone bothered to look into it, several species of Panamanian palms would probably qualify as officially threatened. Concern is mounting, but there is no formal conservation program. Román encourages me to network within Chagres National Park to search for remnant populations. Once we find seeds, we can develop nursery practices and secure samples for the collections at INRENARE's headquarters.

Over the next few weeks, I poll fellow Volunteers when I run into them in the office in Panama City. Stan, an Environmental Education Volunteer, invites Ethan and me to his village for a first palm expedition. He allows that Boquerón Arriba, on the opposite shore of Lake Alajuela, "is just lousy with native palms." We set a date.

In a few weeks Ethan and I set out early for Boquerón Arriba. Like Tranquilla, Boquerón Arriba lies within Chagres National Park, but we have to travel outside the park to get there. Usually the wait for the chiva at Corotú is excruciating. We often sit for hours. The whether-at-all and what-time of the chiva's arrival are consistent only in their uncertainty. By the time it arrives, I am always too tired, too hungry, and too annoyed to pay much attention to the scenery as we make the forty-five-minute drive to La Cabima.

Today we wait only a few minutes. The chiva is crowded, but the driver offers me the passenger seat, and I feel like a celebrity. Ethan hangs off the back. It seems the fare should be reduced for that, but he pays one dollar just like everyone else. From my privileged position, I can take in the landscape. The driver is not in a talkative mood, so we listen to the radio and I look out the window. Our route takes us through the soft greens of the park into the hubbub of a little village and then spits us into a vast red clayscape. A cement factory looms at the center, barely visible through a haze of ocher. No doubt about it. We are headed *afuera* (outside), a term park residents apply to leaving Chagres.

From La Cabima we take a bus north on the Trans-Isthmian Highway to Sardinilla, where we buy warm bottles of orange Fanta. Drunks sneer at us, shouting "gude afernun," a smeared rendition of the one English phrase they know (though it is only nine in the morning). We are still a few hours from our destination, and who knows when the next bus will arrive? A beat-up government truck slows and the driver asks if we want a ride to Salamanca, the next major town. We do not hesitate. The driver helps me into the front seat and chucks the bags into the back. Ethan swings up to ride in the flatbed.

Shortly before we arrive in Salamanca, our driver speeds up to overtake a red pickup truck farther down the road. He leans on the horn and flashes his headlights until the other driver pulls over. The two men exchange a few words, and the driver of the red truck offers to take us as far as Boquerón Abajo, an hour's walk from our ultimate destination of Boquerón Arriba.

As Ethan again swings into the back of the truck, our new escort tells me he is a cattleman. The frayed vinyl seat of the cab cuts at my legs; no matter which way I twist I cannot get comfortable. I am relieved when we finally pull into Boquerón Abajo. The cattleman buys us drinks at the cantina and invites us to visit his finca sometime. We wave noncommitally and thank him as we pull on our packs and start walking. After about an hour, we ask a slight young man on horseback for directions to Boquerón Arriba.

"You are already here," he replies. He dismounts, palms outstretched in a gesture that conveys both "Welcome" and "Duh." The young man's pronouncement feels anticlimactic, and I try not to think about how we've traveled for nearly ten hours on one chiva, one bus, two pickup trucks, and on foot only to end up back in Chagres Park, a few miles from Tranquilla as the crow flies. The young man walks us to Stan's home. The house is closed and dark, so we go next door to inquire at the neighbor's house, which doubles as a small store.

"Ah. Stan will not be delayed long," the storekeeper promises. He tells us he is Stan's landlord and sells us canned tuna and a Hawaiian Punch knock-off. We take the food back to Stan's, where we wait on the porch and wolf it down. Then we pile into his hammock, and when Stan finally arrives he finds us snoozing. He was getting "a few things ready" for the following day, our first nursery project for the native palm seeds.

We are dusty and exhausted from our trip, and it is almost sunset. Stan leads us to the Boquerón River and directs us to a deep swimming hole. We luxuriate in the rare coolness of the water and take in the silhouettes of unfamiliar trees on the bank. As we stand air-drying on the riverbank, night creatures whir and croak their reminders of the jungle we inhabit. Stan's one-room house, though appointed with a cement floor and electricity in the form of a single naked light bulb dangling from the ceiling, is not set up for company. We decide to sleep outside. First we spread out a plastic rain poncho to serve as a mattress and then string a mosquito net over it. We sleep in our clothes.

We wake early after a deep sleep. Stan's landlady cooks us breakfast, as she does for Stan every morning. Must be nice.

"Oh, God, it smells so good in here!" The tuna and punch from the night before were less than satisfying. Stan's landlady serves each of us a fried egg and three perfect *hojaldres* (pieces of Panamanian fry bread). We savor them with cups of syrupy-sweet black coffee and talk over the day's plans.

We will focus on three main palm species: *jira* (stilt palm, *Socratea exorrhiza*), *guagara* (broom palm, *Cryosophila warscewiczii*), and *tagua* (ivory-nut palm, *Phytelephas seemannii*). All three have traditional uses that may no longer be sustainable given the growing human population within the park. By learning more about their life cycle and propagation, we hope to conserve them and sustain their use by park residents.

With its watertight foliage, guagara is especially good for *penca* (palm thatching) for roofs. Jira bark, when stripped from the trunk, makes strong, though gap-ridden, walls and flooring. Jira is one of the most widely used traditional building materials in Chagres National Park. Tagua seeds, about the size of a child's fist, are well suited for carving. Figurines made from the seeds have the feel and sheen of ivory. Both tagua and jira are scarce in our part of the park, but a small supply of guagara persists.

I carry a pouch containing precious guagara seeds spirited from Tranquilla. We set out for the house of the family we will work with for the day. To my surprise, the young man who opens the door is the same one we met the day before on horseback. He looks groggy and equally startled to see us on his threshold. Stan introduces the man as Virgilio. We make small talk, and it becomes clear that Virgilio has no idea why we are here. My irritation mounts as we discern that Stan and Virgilio have previously discussed the palm nursery only in the vaguest terms.

While Stan pretends all is in order, Virgilio miraculously rises to the occasion. He hauls some nice, sandy soil from the river to the proposed nursery site. We fill a few dozen tree bags and plant a seed in each. Virgilio makes quick work of slashing enough saplings to construct a small semillero.

"If INRENARE worked like this, there would be no more problems!" Virgilio exclaims as we stand back to admire our work. These are kind words from someone whose Sunday morning we have disrupted. He thanks us for our efforts with a parting gift of breadfruit and offers to show us where to gather seeds of tagua and jira later that afternoon.

Back at Stan's house, we boil the breadfruit for lunch and enjoy them with a mess of rice. The taste reminds me of the boiled peanuts of my Georgia childhood.

By the time we head back to the forest, it is midafternoon. Virgilio greets us, and now he has his wife and two children in tow. He figures we have about a fifteen-minute walk, tops, to the place where we will gather our palm seeds. An hour later, still in transit, we are mired knee-deep in mud. It is the height of the rainy season and our trail resembles a linear quagmire snaking up the hillside.

"*Allá, arriba*, just a little further," our guide repeats.

We three gringos plod along, emitting vulgar, gassy sounds with the suction of each step, as the agile Virgilio tears ahead. His wife and children keep pace with us, likely from politeness. Barefoot and in seemingly impractical Sunday best, they are immaculate. We are coated in mud.

We brought no food with us and are hopeful when Virgilio scales a *guayaba* (guava, *Psidium guayava*) tree. My mouth waters as I remember the juicy sweetness of a guayaba I tasted months ago in Peace Corps training. But the fruit disappoints. It falls short of ripe and puckers us up rather than refreshing us.

Virgilio is rejuvenated, however, and he announces that we must now leave the trail and bushwhack to his secret spot. He slashes his way down a nearly vertical slope, and we follow. He finds a jira palm and slashes at a small cluster of seeds, barely within reach, a move that yields only a few unpromising green nuggets. We bag these and concentrate on the prospect of more to come. Virgilio continues his descent until we no longer hear the swinging of his machete. Returning after around twenty minutes, he sheepishly opens his hands to reveal a single armored tagua seed in each outstretched palm.

Virgilio suggests I stay behind with his wife and children while he and Ethan scramble up another steep slope. A while later, Ethan yells they have found another jira palm but will have to chop it down in order collect the seeds. I consider this just a few seconds too long and yell back that they should spare the tree. This directive is followed by a thud. The tree has already been sacrificed. The woodsmen return with a paltry two dozen or so seeds. They look like a cluster of small pecans and cling grape-like to a gnarled lattice of stems. We drop them into the bag.

Virgilio wants to use the bark of the fallen jira and will return to collect it and haul it back to the village. So, in our efforts to save the native palms of Panamá, we have unwittingly hastened their extirpation.

We descend the hill. Virgilio asks what the chances are of the Peace Corps giving him a tin roof for his chicken coop. With so little guagara, after all, there is not much in the way of roofing material. I change the subject by making a conversational toast to the success of Virgilio's new nursery.

"*Si Dios quiere*" (If God wills it), he concedes.

III

Sapling (Establishment)
July–December 1992

14

Recursos Naturales

With a few small tree nursery and reforestation projects launched, I learn that July is the *Mes de Recursos Naturales* (Natural Resources Month). Gladys asks me to write a song or a poem to be presented by one of Tranquilla's children at the multischool celebration to be held in a few weeks.

Earth Day is probably the closest thing to Natural Resources Month that we have in the United States. I tried unsuccessfully to introduce the concept back in April as *Día de la Tierra* (Day of the Earth), wherein I barged into the school with a potted tree announcing, "We will now plant this." The bewildered children cooperated, but not surprisingly the meaning of the occasion escaped them. Elated over this chance to redeem myself, I fully embrace the spirit of the season and apply myself to the task Gladys has assigned me.

The Spanish word *recurso* (resource) sounds a lot like the English word "recourse." A few days later, by the regretful expression on Gladys's face, I see that recourse is precisely what she feels she lacks. I want to disappear under her contemptuous glare as I sing for her my masterpiece. The lyrics to "This Land Is Your Land," although winsome in my own tongue, apparently do not translate into Spanish very well. Plaintive, I assure Gladys that I will get back to her later with better material, and I slink home.

The next morning, I scrap the song and embark on an entirely different creative venture—a poem. English-to-Spanish dictionary in hand, I scratch down line by line, chew my pencil, write a little more, then strike out several lines and begin again. Juana staggers by and asks to borrow the cayuco.

"Sorry, Juana. Ethan needs to use it to go get firewood." Although it is true, we do need firewood and Ethan does plan to go get some today, my guilty conscience knows I likely would not lend the boat to Juana anyway.

She is too unstable, both physically and mentally, and I cannot be sure she will return the boat.

"Maria. I need to go fishing. If you do not lend me your cayuco I will die of hunger." I have come to expect such melodrama from Juana. Still, there is that nagging guilt. I suggest she ask another neighbor, one that does not need to use his boat this afternoon. I accompany Juana to ask at our next-door neighbor's house. They tell her no. We get the same response at the next house. Juana wanders off cursing. I go back to my poem, and a while later Ethan goes for firewood. He returns with the news that he spotted Juana out fishing, so someone finally lent her a boat after all.

I proudly recite my poem for Gladys a few days later. Not only did I manage to make it rhyme—in Spanish, no less—but I actually squeezed in some interesting facts about sedimentation, watersheds, and deforestation. Gladys nods in approval and calls over Nelida, the star pupil of the sixth grade, who will recite it. To my dismay, Gladys announces that she will work with Nelida on pairing an arrangement of *mimicos* (hand motions) to go with each line of the poem. The thought fills me with dread. Mimicos are stilted, rehearsed gestures that serve as a dramatization for recitations of all kinds. In spite of their ridiculousness, they are abhorrently common in school performances. My mild protest takes the form of questioning aloud whether mimicos are really necessary. Gladys points out that everyone will be doing them, and that Nelida's chances of winning the competition are slim if she abstains. It is hard to argue with that logic.

Nelida begins work on memorizing and reciting the poem, and I begin scheming. It occurs to me that Gladys now owes me a favor. After school one afternoon, I call her attention to the footpath between Tranquilla and Quebrada Benitez and suggest a tree-planting project. It seems everyone has an idea for how to capitalize on Natural Resources Month. For example, Gladys was also approached recently by the Ministry of Agriculture about planting a school garden as part of the month-long celebration. After all, food is a natural resource too. We decide on a three-pronged celebration for Tranquilla with planting trees early in the month, starting a school garden in mid-July, and staging the lakewide celebration as the month closes.

As for the tree planting, it is largely a symbolic gesture. Seldom used, the path between Tranquilla and Quebrada Benitez is downright treacherous in places. Most travelers prefer to paddle between the two villages. Many segments also lack shade. With underuse and a lack of maintenance, shrubs and paja mala also encroach on many areas, a safety concern given that most walk the path in bare feet and there are poisonous snakes about.

Gladys and I decide to plant 129 seedlings, one for every man, woman, and child in Tranquilla. Make that 130 with the recent birth of Señor Lorenzo's new grandchild. We opt to plant *gmelina* (white beech, *Gmelina arborea*). Although introduced to Panamá from Eurasia, gmelina is well suited for row plantings and often used along boulevards and pathways.

For a rural school in Panamá, arranging a field trip is as simple as setting the date with the teacher. Back home we would have all kinds of parental supervision, permission slips, and liability waivers. Here, at the nod of the teacher we are set to escort twenty-two elementary schoolchildren through snake-infested brush.

In preparation, Ethan and I preselect the length of trail along which the planting will occur. We clear the trail right up to that point so the children may pass safely. We also clear and prepare the planting sites. We figure the smaller kids might plant up to five trees, the bigger ones as many as ten.

Early on the appointed morning, Ethan and I harvest young gmelina seedlings from a well-established grove behind the village store and load them into two borrowed motetes. I carefully prepare the drinking water, which I will personally carry. The kids are tough, but I worry about overheating and dehydration. I lack the time needed to boil the water. Concerned about sanitation, I instead add a few drops of chlorine bleach, one of the methods recommended in the Army safety manual for treating drinking water. Our preparations complete, we walk to the school and enter the classroom, where we find the children already at their desks.

"*Buenos días*, Maria. *Buenos días*, Etan," sing the children upon Gladys's prompting. Each child sips from a plastic cup of *crema* (rice cereal). I think of crema as vile, soupy stuff, but the children's opinion seems to differ from my own—and many of them likely arrived at school hungry this morning. In anticipation of the day's exertion, Gladys arranged for some of the mothers to arrive early to prepare this modest breakfast. The children beam and tilt their heads way back to work every last dribble of crema from the cups.

After the meal, we pick up the motetes and set off for the hills. Our various gaits sort us into little bunches. Gladys, in her lipstick, big jewelry, and baseball cap, sways and sachets with her girly entourage at a leisurely pace near the back. Ethan's stride is purposeful as he leads the way and carries one motete on his back. The oldest boy is eager to separate himself from the younger students and carries the other motete, close on Ethan's heels. The youngest kids skip, run, and bound up the hill full of limitless, if undirected, energy. Each wields a pick, shovel, or machete. I schlep the water jug while ploddingly bringing up the rear.

At the top of the hill, before we reach the planting area, it is time for a preemptive drink. We pass around the cups and portion out the specially prepared, parasite-free water. I swig separately from a canteen.

Several of the children spit their water out on the ground. I think nothing of it until one of the older girls approaches me and says quietly, "Maria, *el agua es cómo mál* [the water tastes bad]." I dismiss the comment as ungrateful whining.

Ethan asks, "Did you bring any other water?"

"No. We'll just have to make it last all morning."

"What I mean is this stuff is undrinkable." He holds out a cup for me to try and I spit it out in round measure. It has a chlorine taste much more intense than that of a swimming pool. I am horrified and make a round of apologies. It becomes clear that the main worry weighing on the children's minds is that I may insist they drink it anyway. Cheers follow as I tell the children to pour the water onto the ground. A couple of girls collect the cups.

With no drinking water, I ask Gladys if we should turn back.

"Normally they go all day working in the hot sun with their parents and never drink a drop. We'll be back at the school in less than two hours anyway. Why turn back now?"

We arrive at the planting area, and kids organize around the small clearings that designate each planting site. As adults shuttle seedlings, bigger children dig the holes, and smaller ones use their hands to fill each hole with soil. We show them how to tamp down the earth and give each seedling a little tug to ensure it is secure in its new home. Accustomed to hard work, the students are quickly done with the task. They scamper along the path and soon we are back at the school. We had no water for the newly planted trees, so I am thankful for the onset of the rains that continue throughout the afternoon.

A few days later, a technician from the Ministry of Agriculture arrives with garden plans and materials. He introduces himself as Jorge Hernández. Something about his stocky build and overgroomed mustache makes me feel uneasy—or maybe it is the way he ogles me. He foists several packets of expired vegetable seeds at me and then launches into a short classroom lecture on nutrition. Jorge leads the group to the new school garden plot, recently cleared by several of the parents upon Gladys's request.

Although the well-dressed Jorge seems a bit too prissy for this sort of work, the children again are impressive in their know-how, focus, and strength. We are hard at work heeling in a row of pineapple tops when Jorge makes his move.

Salamando—improvising lyrics in the traditional way—he weaves a ballad about a fetching young gringa sent to Panamá to toy with his heart. The gringa's beauty is unequaled, but he knows not where he stands. His song rambles on. Several of the girls start giggling. The boys take no notice, some digging frantically, others drawing in the soil with sticks.

I feel the flush on my skin spreading to the crown of my head when Gladys hisses, "For the love of God, Jorge, can you not see you are embarrassing Maria?"

Undeterred, Jorge goes on to make veiled references to what might happen in a future, private setting. I blurt, "*Quita se* [Cut it out]!" I throw down my hoe and stomp off.

Later, as I talk with Gladys, she is completely blasé about Jorge's behavior. There are no sexual harassment laws on the books in Panamá. If there were they would not be enforced. Machismo is rampant in the culture. Although she intervened in the moment, now she fails to see his comportment as anything more than a slight annoyance.

I am still mulling over harassment in this new context when the grand celebration is upon us: Natural Resources Day, the culmination of all our hard work and creativity. Gabi's husband shuttles Tranquilla's elementary students to nearby Victoriano Lorenzo in the new UCLA cayuco. The children's excitement is palpable.

The occasion itself is something of a letdown. Local officials (among them Jorge, whom I manage to avoid) drone on with their interminable speeches. The speeches finally give way to the talent show, but by then everyone is so hungry it is hard to pay attention. All things considered, Nelida's performance is brilliant. She wears a slightly-too-short yellow gingham dress that accentuates her long, skinny legs. In her mimicos, she alternates between reaching up to the sky beseechingly, bending down on her knees as if in prayer, and putting her wrist to her forehead, all while belting out the lines of the poem. She wins first place among the sixth graders.

She is aglow at lunchtime and eats a generous helping of *arroz con pollo* (rice with chicken) surrounded by several young fans. We return to Tranquilla triumphant and happy.

15

Donde el Gringo

"*El Gringo* was here looking for you." I look up from the paper in front of me, a sheet on which I have been scribbling furiously about ProTec's latest antics. I stare at the youth who delivers this message and recognize him as one of the new members of the farmers' cooperative.

I decide to find out where he stands in the whole thing. "ProTec! They bring in their poisons and fertilizers and think they can get away with it!" He could not look more surprised. I go on to rant about the perils of inadequate training. And doesn't he agree, after all, that complicating the plantain project with synthetic chemicals will merely create an unhealthy dependency? And the likelihood that villagers will give up on such a project goes without saying. The youth becomes surly.

"We have not either given up on the project. We cleaned the field all day yesterday. Tomorrow we fertilize the sick plants and remove the dead leaves." He pauses before continuing, recovering some of his reverence for el Gringo.

"Anyway, *su compadre* [your comrade] says you can live in his house *pues* [then]. He'll be back in a few weeks to arrange things."

"Arrange things," I scoff. El Gringo assumes much. Moreover, I take offense that my neighbors assume I am pals with el Gringo just because we both happen to be North American. The youngster vanishes.

Tranquilla draws a distinction between *un* gringo (a gringo), any North American, and *el* Gringo (*the* Gringo). For Ethan and me, el Gringo has taken on a mythical quality. All we know of him is that he constructed an ostentatious—by Tranquilla's standards—lakeshore home on the outskirts of the village. Built about a decade ago, the house now serves as a monument to the grandeur of el Gringo himself. Elegant in whitewashed coolness, the stucco walls rise gracefully from the concrete floor to the tiled roof. Although it was abandoned immediately after completion, the structure's solidity mocks Tranquilla's fleeting ranchos with their walls of bark and roofs of palm.

The mere presence of such a house in that location remains an enigma. After all, it is illegal to build a new home within the boundary of a national park. Although the park guards might overlook the ranchos of a few dozen squatters, a permanent dwelling is another matter. And why would el Gringo select a muddy cove in a campesino village as a getaway spot?

No doubt the place was destined to have its own grand name, Hacienda Tranquila (Tranquil Estates), for example. Never inhabited, it became simply Donde el Gringo (The Gringo's Place). People routinely pass through the yard as a shortcut to the village center, undeterred by the surrounding fence of rusted barbed wire.

I ponder a vine snake weaving through the shaggy thatch of my kitchen ceiling. It is the rainy season. I shiver in my short sleeves and curse the rancho's open design. The rains have dampened the firewood. The kitchen floor is just plain nasty and is getting nastier. Water seeps through it, creating a muddy veneer. I have placed pots on the floor to collect the worst trickles from the largest gaps in the thinning roof. I curl my toes farther into my sandals. In short, I am tempted by el Gringo's offer.

Temptation shames me. Living in a traditional rancho at the edge of a vast jungle initially fulfilled my long-held dream about Peace Corps service. But the rain has melted away much of the charm, and the chance to toss this hut aside for a comfortable existence at Donde el Gringo becomes an obsession. I fantasize about waking up to dry feet below and an absence of snakes above. I dream of evenings surrounded by solid walls that clearly delineate where lamplight ends and the jungle night begins. Donde el Gringo begins to symbolize a place of security and peacefulness.

I am tempted further when two women I have never seen before approach the house. They are nicely dressed, and one of them carries a book and a handful of pamphlets. I'm intrigued by them at first but quickly realize they are here to evangelize.

"*Buenos días, señora,*" they begin their spiel politely. Of all the stresses I anticipated living in a remote village in the Panamanian countryside, persecution by the Jehovah's Witnesses did not even make the list. The shock of their visit at first renders me speechless. Then rage overcomes me, and speechlessness yields to ineloquent sputtering: "You and you! Leave now! I no care in what you have say!"

The Jehovah's Witnesses love a challenge, and I am clearly possessed of some evil they believe they are responsible for excising. They do not leave. My utterances become more inarticulate the longer they stay, and I finally go inside and slam the door, a futile gesture considering I can hear them just as well inside as out. They continue reading their material, thank me, and finally go along to the next house. Had I been living at el Gringo's at the time, going inside and closing the door would have been much more effective. I wasn't and it wasn't, but I could change that.

I tell Ethan about the Jehovah's Witnesses as we carry mugs of tea to el Gringo's at dusk. We trail clouds of chamomile and step gingerly through the fence, careful not to spill the hot liquid. The feathery shapes of *paraques*, native birds similar to whippoorwills, flutter over the untended shrubbery, barely visible in the growing darkness. Their eerie chortles beckon us deeper onto the property.

El Gringo's muelle offers a perfect sunset view, but tropical sunsets are overrated. Here the sun is all business, disappearing below the horizon like a watch dropping into a pocket. Proximity to the equator snuffs out the color almost as soon as it erupts. We agonize over what we assume is our decision to make. Should we move here, or should we not?

We repeat this evening ritual for a few days. I develop an elaborate rationalization of being an equally effective Peace Corps Volunteer whether living in el Gringo's house or a rancho.

"I mean, we can live in a hut all we want, but that won't exactly make us Panamanians," I hear myself say to my beloved. "Living at *el Gringo*'s wouldn't do us any more damage than being gringos in the first place." The Peace Corps's sensible requirement that Volunteers live at or below the level of the community does not factor into the discussion at this early stage.

I lose perspective during these deliberations, initially failing to see the irony of context. Back home in the United States, this temptress of a house would have little appeal. Set on a Florida lakeside its few rooms of spare concrete would be rustic, just a step above camping. In an urban setting, its scrawny carapace would be deemed blight and likely condemned. But in Tranquilla it is a mansion.

As the weeks wear on, our dithering gives way to a more honest consideration of what Donde el Gringo symbolizes to the people of Tranquilla. It is the constant, nagging presence of the United States, puppeteer of the Panamanian government. It is a lifestyle the people of Chagres National Park can never hope to achieve. Most of all, Donde el Gringo is an outpost of otherness in the community. Only an outsider would place such an incongruous structure in the midst of a subsistence community. Only an outsider would choose to live there.

Ethan grabs a shovel one morning and digs a trench, eighteen inches deep, on the uphill side of the kitchen.

"Oh my God! Come look at this!" He has unearthed a giant worm, at least as long as the trench is deep. We are fascinated in a grossed-out kind of way and marvel at its purple skin and snakelike size.

Within a few days, the trench seems to be working. It has rerouted the water so that now our kitchen floor seems at least as dry as everyone else's. We sit over a lunch of fried yuca and consider the virtues of our little rancho. It is centrally located, it is not surrounded by barbed wire, and our meager ten dollars in monthly rent provides income to a campesino family that needs the money.

While we chat, a young neighbor approaches the house. His hands are cupped together and he walks carefully. He opens his hands like a clamshell and reveals a tiny winged creature, eyes huge and staring. Two younger siblings follow.

"It fell from its nest!" explains the younger brother.

Ethan examines it as the impossibly tiny hummingbird attempts to make itself look even smaller.

"Put it back, Etan!" begs the younger girl.

Together, we walk up the hill to the mango tree where the empty nest sits on a branch just barely above eye level. Ethan climbs partway up the tree to look more closely at the nest. At one time the nest might have contained two eggs, possibly even two tiny chicks. But if the fledgling were placed back into the nest it would spill uncomfortably over the sides.

"It's too big for the nest," Ethan explains as he descends the tree. "The little chick outgrew his home. It was time. The mother is probably nearby."

"But it can't even fly!" they protest.

"Of course not. Don't worry. The parents will teach it."

The oldest boy places the fledgling back at the base of the tree trunk, where he originally found it. They leave.

We continue our conversation and decide to stay put. I think we both feel a little embarrassed that we considered moving to el Gringo's. We have the rest of our lives to live in luxury by global standards. Our choice should have been as decisive as a tropical sunset. Fortunately, el Gringo never returns to test our resolve.

16

La Operación

I sit at my kitchen table, contemplating the lake as it fills with afternoon rain. I mull over my uninspiring dinner options, variations on a starch-based theme. Weighing the pros and cons of rice with plantain versus plantain with rice, I look up to see Gabi smiling at me, a welcome distraction.

"*Buenas*, Maria."

"*Buenas tardes* [good afternoon], Gabi."

She settles on the rough bench of my kitchen. I scramble to provide refreshment, as Gabi always does when I visit her rancho. Fortunately, the tree right next to the kitchen has a few ripe oranges within reach. These I slice and squeeze into enamel mugs. The flavor is a watery essence, and several dashes of sugar are in order. Having abandoned any attempts at water purification after nearly poisoning Tranquilla's schoolchildren last month, I dispense water straight from the spigot into each mug. After a quick stir of the weak solution with a pocked teaspoon, I hand the chicha to my friend and sit on the bench beside her.

"*Mira* [look], Maria," she says as she takes the mug. "I came to ask you a favor." She falters, lowering her eyes. "I am going to the hospital so they can operate on me. So I have no more babies." She is asking me to help her obtain a tubal ligation.

I am astonished. Although contraceptives are available in Panama City, birth control is generally discouraged in this Catholic nation. Here in the countryside, family planning is never discussed. In rural areas, tradition dictates producing children in quantity. Large families are still perceived as an economic asset in subsistence farming communities like Tranquilla. As a foreigner, I decided at the beginning of my Peace Corps service to avoid the issue of reproductive health. I chose to compartmentalize my concern about the global population explosion and respect cultural norms, no matter how much I disagreed with them.

I try to think of this moment as simply a chance to support a friend. For whatever reason, Gabi has decided that a tenth child would be one too many. Her decision is brave, modern, and entirely her own. I cannot bring myself to ask her what first comes to mind, whether her husband, Augusto, knows her plans. Instead I offer, "What do you need, then?"

"*Bueno*. I go to Santo Tomás, the public hospital, in Panama City. They don't charge anything, but patients have to bring their own blood donor. I wondered if you could be my donor, pues."

"And if we are not the same blood type?"

"*No importa* [Not important]. The main thing is they need a donor to help some other patient. That way, they always have enough." I reason through this as she continues. "My appointment is on Thursday. *Puede acompañarme* [Could you accompany me]?"

"Do you think they'll accept blood from a *gringa* foreigner?"

"They say they will." She has obviously been thinking about this for some time, of me in particular, even. I suppose this is not surprising. Gabi knows that I am not plugged into Tranquilla's circle of gossip. My complicity would make this so much simpler.

"Thursday it is. What time do we leave?"

At dawn, Augusto ferries us across the lake. His face is lined and sullen, but I am still uncertain whether he knows the purpose of our journey. On the chiva and bus into the city, Gabi and I pass the time chitchatting and dozing.

We arrive at the central bus station, and Gabi falters. Although she visited the hospital recently, the tangle of crowded streets and alleys confuses her. We zig this way, zag another, increasingly disoriented as we go. Gabi seems to have left her usual air of confidence in Tranquilla. She clings to me every time we cross the street. Although she is the citizen and I the foreigner, I am more comfortable than she in this urban setting. Finally, I hail a taxi. We tell the driver we are headed to Santo Tomás. He gets us there safely and on time and charges only one dollar. As I pay, I notice Gabi's scandalized expression. The average campesino might earn five dollars for a full day's work. For less than ten minutes of his time, I paid the driver more than her husband could have earned in two hours of hard labor.

Santo Tomás is a complex of several buildings, each with its own specialty.

The cinder-block construction hints at a humanitarian aid project gone stale. We step through the dark corridors, lights off to save on electricity. In fact, throughout the complex, only the barest minimum of electricity is in use. We navigate around stretchers, children wrapped in blankets, and wasted forms abandoned in wheelchairs. Rooms lining the corridor resemble monastic cells. Some contain one or more patients. Others house curious mixtures of medical and office equipment. We finally locate the waiting area, check in, and find seats together. Our tension deteriorates into boredom as we run out of things to talk about.

A nurse finally calls my name. The staff is courteous, never once remarking on my nationality or accent. They do not ask for identification, only that I fill out a few simple forms. A masked nurse looks over the paperwork and draws a blood sample to determine whether I will be a suitable donor. She disappears into an adjoining lab.

As we wait to learn the results, Gabi and I are back to laughing and joking in the waiting room. The nurse returns. "Your iron is a little low."

Well, that explains a lot. I have suffered from anemia on and off since adolescence. Lately, I have had little energy and have needed ten to twelve hours of sleep every night. The unvaried, starch-based diet has taken its toll. I appreciate her concern for my health, but we are here to discuss Gabi.

The nurse's tone fails to obscure her annoyance that I do not grasp the significance of her report. "I'm afraid this means you are not eligible as a blood donor."

I leave the room dazed, dejected, speechless. Gabi follows, her smile now vanished. I avoid looking at her for fear I will see her cry or start crying myself. When I finally do look, Gabi is wiping a cheek on one sleeve. The other cheek still glistens. I look away again and we retrace our steps back through the hospital, both of us staring straight ahead. We arrive at the exit, where a steady downpour intimidates us. I open my umbrella, and we scrunch together to keep dry. We start walking, unsure of a destination and not quite ready to go back to the bus stop.

"Do you like pizza?" I ask desperately in front of a little Italian restaurant.

"Never tried it," she replies. In we go, and I order a large.

"Okay. We need a backup plan. I was anemic before, and my doctor gave me iron pills to help. I'll pick some up from the clinic and get better." Gabi still looks glum, and tears collect once more. She dabs at her eyes with the corner of a paper napkin she has been alternately twisting and shredding.

"Gabi. I'll take the pills, and then we'll go back to the hospital. You can get your operation then. See? It will be fine."

The pizza arrives, and Gabi bites into hers, tentatively at first, then with enthusiasm. "This stuff is tasty."

We distract ourselves with more polite conversation about her children. Her youngest son plans to spend the summer in the Interior at his teacher's house. Her youngest daughter has milk teeth, which ache as they rot away. Her oldest daughter's fifteenth birthday is coming up, one important enough in this culture that it has its own name: the *quinceañera*, or "sweet fifteen."

Gabi wraps the leftovers in what is left of her napkin to take to Augusto. "So he can try it too," she explains.

Back in Tranquilla, I begin an iron-boosting regimen. I put the word out that I will buy fresh fish for breakfast and lunch, and the children drop it by regularly. For evening meals, I keep seco salado on hand, the dried and salted fish a bargain at fifty cents per pound. Canned tuna and dried red beans serve as backups. I never turn down a chance to eat chicken at a neighbor's house or community gathering. Full of optimism, I plant a row of *espinaca* (vine spinach, *Basella alba*) in my kitchen garden.

A few weeks later, I feel much improved and suggest to Gabi that we make another go of it. She looks sheepish, then confides, "*Ya estoy del estado*" (I am already in the state). She is pregnant again. I want to comfort her, tell her we will find a way, but her tone and facial expression tell me she considers the discussion closed.

Puzzled, I describe the situation to the Peace Corps nurse on my next trip to the city. He explains that tubal ligations cannot be performed without risk to the developing fetus. Abortion is highly restricted in Panamá, permitted only in cases of rape or incest, or if the mother's life is in danger. Endangering a fetus is certainly not an option; therefore Gabi is not a candidate for the operation—at least for several months.

I survey my row of spinach. Some plants flourish, while others languish, themselves looking as though they could use a good iron supplement. With luck, Gabi's pregnancy will go well. Her tenth child will appear just before my return to the United States. I gather a handful of the healthiest leaves to take to my newly expecting friend. The rest I toss into my dinner bowl, where they lend a bitter crunch to the bland backdrop of tonight's rice.

17

Victor Venenoso

I finally make it back to the Peace Corps office, and Justin says he has something for me. He closes his office door behind me and hands me the letter he received earlier in the week from ProTec's Latin America director.

While remaining diplomatic, the letter was very direct. The director took our allegations seriously. I had written the letter in English, so she translated it into Spanish before discussing it personally with Pimentél, who then followed up with the ProTec advisor assigned to the UCLA to hear his side of the story. She gently chastised us for not establishing a professional relationship with Pimentél. As ProTec's country director, she said he would be receptive to the issues we raised.

Justin makes a copy for me. I fret over the contents, all of which ring true. We should have looked for a more local solution, strengthening bridges rather than burning them down.

"ProTec was pissed at what they called our 'misdirected complaint,'" says Justin. So much so that Pimentél initially refused to grant us an appointment. In the face of that obstruction, Justin went to the ProTec office and knocked on Pimentél's door. As he put it, that meeting was simply a matter of absorbing Pimentél's wrath in order to make a more productive meeting possible in the future. UCLA's ProTec advisor had written a four-page letter full of rage, most of it personal and fired directly at me.

"It was clear he was just trying to cover his ass," Justin tries to reassure me. Still, he doesn't permit me to see the letter.

"We'll be meeting with ProTec and the park staff next week. Meet me here at the office. We'll walk over together." Sensing my anxiety, he wraps up with "You may feel like you're in the hot seat. But remember, you're justified."

I spend the night in town before the appointed date and meet Justin at the office as planned. My feet drag, and my perspiration is impressive. As we walk to the offices of ProTec I am in a fog of nerves and humidity. Román waits at ProTec's entrance. I greet him as warmly as a clammy handshake will permit. He shrinks against the wall when I ask him how he's holding up.

"*Aquí, más o menos* [I've been better], Maria." In that moment, I wonder if I have let him down. How much worse did we make things with that letter?

Next arrives Francisco, president of UCLA, straight from the countryside. He wears cutarras and a sombrero, every inch the campesino, and carries a canvas bag over his shoulder. Unlike many farmers, Francisco is as comfortable in the boardrooms of the capital city as he is in the fields of the campo. Normally our relationship is easy, but today it is clear that he is ProTec's star character witness, and his greeting is curt. Although he barely glances at me, he shakes hands with Justin and Román.

Pimentél keeps us waiting for half an hour, *just to show us who's boss*, I think darkly.

Finally, we are ushered into the room and take our seats around the conference table. Pimentél blows right by the introductions, launching into an impassioned description of ProTec's good works. The preamble has its intended effect and actually softens me a bit. They have, after all, brought many wonderful solutions to rural Panamá, including solar dryers for papaya and seco salado, and a connection to city markets.

Román listens respectfully to Pimentél's speech and then gently takes control of the meeting. "Thank you, everyone, for coming to discuss the policy on the use of agricultural chemicals within the national park system. Your attendance today shows your support of our agency and a willingness to work together. As you know, we have a very clear policy prohibiting the use of chemicals in Chagres National Park. What we have trouble with is enforcement. Here we need your help."

With these few sentences, Román has made heroes of us all, shifting the focus away from the misdeeds committed by ProTec and putting us on the same team. In other words, he has cleaned up the mess that Justin and I created with our confrontational approach.

There are two sides to the issue, says Pimentél: the human side and the desire to protect our resources. Unable to keep quiet, I go on the defensive while maintaining my voice as level as possible. Of course campesinos must feed their families, and growing food means effective pest control. I fear we are headed down a path requiring heavy chemical inputs that are not in balance with community needs, like clean drinking water, or with the park's conservation goals. We have to explore other options to manage pests and improve production.

To my astonishment, Francisco chimes in to support me. "We are talking about a *medio de vida* [way of life], no? One that is consistent with protecting the environment. Our practices have to be both profitable and sustainable."

After these interjections, Román reminds us that the sale or use of agricultural chemicals within the national park is prohibited, although in rare instances a variance may be granted.

"Oh, well, naturally we will provide the needed documentation," blurts Pimentél. All eyes are upon him as he backpedals. "If we were ever to find a need to use chemicals. Hypothetically, no?"

"Good. That would be consistent with *La Norma Químico en Cuenca, Ley 39*." Román, ever the bureaucrat, nods approvingly while citing the pertinent regulation.

As we continue talking, we all agree that environmental education has a key role to play. For now, we will collaborate on integrated pest management approaches for the region's farmers. In the long term, we will work with the school system to pilot an environmental education program.

Months later, a neighbor's children sit at my kitchen table poring through old *Newsweek* magazines, exclaiming over photos of world events. In the fashion section, "*Eso, sí es feo*" (That one sure is ugly). In the postelection coverage, "*Mira*, Presidente Bill Clinton!" We hear footsteps and look up to see Román smiling at us.

He asks the kids how they are doing. "*Qué pasa?*"

My seven-year-old visitor excitedly describes the puppet show, *Victor Venenoso* (*Poisonous Victor*), which Ethan and I had put on at the school a few days before.

"Victor is this bad guy, see? And he sells poison to the village. Victor said it would help the crops grow. But then the parents used it, and the kids, everybody got sick. Some of them were real sick and had to go to the hospital."

A cloud of alarm passes across Román's face, and I quickly realize that the boy has not mentioned the words "puppet show." I explain that *Victor Venenoso* is part of the new environmental education curriculum we are trying out in the school, and I produce Victor himself, a hooded puppet clothed in black. I recite a few lines from the puppet show, and Román laughs.

18

Salud

I wish she would stop doing that! Señora Catalina's silent arrivals continue to startle me. Today she materializes as I linger over coffee dregs, considering whether to make another pot. She summons me to the house of her brother-in-law. He has an infection of some kind and she wants me to take a look at it.

Word of my Peace Corps–issued medical kit hit the street some months ago, so the request is not unusual. I always attend to such patients with trepidation. The Peace Corps made it clear early on that our first-aid supplies are for personal use only, but I do not know of a single Volunteer who does not dispense them to "Host Country Nationals" in times of need.

I take my supplies to his house and find the man sitting in a hammock, his right big toe grotesquely swollen. It was punctured while he was working barefoot to clear a field for planting. I soak the foot in clean, warm water and apply hydrogen peroxide to the wound, which grows pale and indistinct. He flinches as the cleanser bubbles. I grab a cotton bandage and slather antibacterial ointment onto it. I wrap the injured toe in the bandage and give him a half dozen more lengths of the gauze. "Keep these. Change them daily. Throw the old one away; do not reuse it. Apply fresh cream three times a day. You must keep it clean and dry." I am terse in part because I do not have a strong health-care vocabulary, but also in part from my concern over the state of his foot. In this climate, a simple infection can become a life-and-death issue.

The family gives me a clear wine bottle corked with a corncob and filled with *nance* (golden spoon, *Byrsonima crassifolia*) berries packed in water. *Chicha de nance* (sweet nance beverage) is one of my favorites, a nonalcoholic drink completely lacking an analogue back in the United States.

Back at my rancho, I pour a few of the fruits into a cup, mash them with my fingers, and then remove the stony pits. The fruit is waxy and fatty. I add sugar and water to the pulp and mix. The resulting beverage resembles a tangy-sweet kefir (albeit a nondairy version) and I gulp it down.

As I prepare a second serving, I reflect on the difficulties of cultivating a conservation ethic among people who lack access to even basic first-aid supplies. Campesinos piece their lives together day by day as it is. I think about a recent snakebite death in Quebrada Ancha, the widespread cholera outbreak, the deplorable condition of people's teeth. The need for preventive health care among my neighbors is clear. Maybe Tranquilla residents would be more open to discussing conservation if they could first make some tangible gains in their daily health?

Although my program is forestry—not health—I wonder whether establishing a health committee could be an answer to some of Tranquilla's needs, and ultimately a conduit to environmental conservation. From education to drinking water and farming, it seems there is a committee for everything in Tranquilla. How were health and basic first aid missed?

With the threat of cholera, the need for latrines in the community seems most pressing of all. Although relatively isolated from the epicenter of the cholera outbreak, villagers defecate wherever they have the urge and can get a little privacy—in the woods, behind a shed, anywhere. In a concentrated population, the danger of diseases spreading is severe. By comparison, I am relatively lucky. I have access to an old latrine left over from the days when the family of Señor Patricio's oldest son lived here. However, it is quickly filling, and I worry it will soon overflow. All this lack of sanitation is bound to run downhill to the lake.

I approach a few community leaders with my idea—a health committee—and a concrete example of a first project: the latrinization of the community. Señor Patricio is receptive but is doubtful about finding someone to lead the group. It must be someone who is not already in a leadership position.

"What about Manuel?" I ask.

Well liked and respected by his peers, Manuel seems a natural choice. He is Señora Catalina's son from a previous marriage and looks to be about my age. He is muscular and tall and works hard—when he feels like it. Patricio suggests Manuel is something of a layabout. "But give it a try. It would be good for him."

I thank him and turn to leave. Then I have an idea. "Señor Patricio. Do you like pizza?" After seeing how much Gabi enjoyed the pizza in Panama

City, I thought I should investigate how widespread the lack of pizza consumption was in Tranquilla.

"Pizza. Heard about it. Never tried it, though."

"Well, you've got the oven and you know how to make dough you can use for the crust. If I bring you some ingredients, will you make us some pizza?"

"*Cómo no* [We'll see], Maria."

A few days later Manuel is working at the tienda. I approach him with my proposal. "Señor Patricio thinks you could make a great leader of this group. How about it?"

His mouth bunches under his robust mustache and he assumes the expression that often precedes one of his jokes. He is just about to brush me off with a lighthearted jest but then catches himself. He turns his attention to one of Gabi's tiny children, who wants to purchase twenty-five cents worth of kerosene.

After the child leaves, Manuel says "*Bien* [Very well]. Who else should we invite, pues?"

We discuss a handful of potential candidates and decide to gather for the first time as a committee the following weekend. During the ensuing week, Manuel will inform the others, and I will travel to Salamanca to check into the availability of free or low-cost latrine supplies at the Ministry of Health outpost.

Ethan and I set out together for Salamanca, about ten miles north on the Trans-Isthmian Highway. On arriving at Corotú, we learn that the chiva is not running today—it operates only when the driver is in the mood. Today is the only day that will work this week for the fact-finding mission. So we must hitchhike if we are going to make it—not a likely prospect with so little traffic. Still—if we walk partway out with no luck, we'll be back in Tranquilla by sunset.

We start up the dusty road. It is a hot, dry day. Fortunately, we have a light load in our packs, as it is only a day trip. We trudge along for about an hour, and my breakfast wears off. I'd planned to be in La Cabima by now, buying tortillas and coffee before the next leg of our journey. The temperature is rising. It must be at least ninety-five degrees, and it's only ten thirty in the morning. I'm having second thoughts when we hear the rumblings of a vehicle approaching. It is very quiet at first, and we are not quite sure we have properly diagnosed the sound. As it approaches, the crunching of gravel beneath the tires is more insistent. We might have a shot at a ride after all.

A flash of orange, the large truck emerges from a cloud of dust. Two men ride in the cab. Self-conscious about sticking our thumbs out for a ride, we do so nonetheless to make our need clear. The truck slows to a stop.

"Where are you headed?" The passenger asks.

"Only as far as La Cabima. The chiva isn't running today. Don't suppose we could have a ride?"

"Hop in; we're on our way to Panama City, so we have to pass through Cabima anyway."

He opens the door, and rather than scooting over to make room for us in the spacious cab, he gets out. That's when we see it. Our host is wielding a machine gun. Ethan and I exchange a glance. Then, trying to appear as comfortable around automatic weapons as possible, we climb into the cab.

Have we just been taken hostage? Is this how it happens?

We bump and bounce along the decrepit road to La Cabima. We attempt to make small talk with our hosts, hoping to prove that we often find ourselves hitching rides from heavily armed men. We find them furtive, though, and receive only an occasional response from the driver. Meanwhile, the man riding "shotgun" nervously monitors the scenery out the window, gun carefully poised and ready for action. We notice both men are perspiring profusely, a bad case of nerves.

Twenty minutes later we are in La Cabima and the truck rolls to a halt. They let us off as promised, and we are giddy with relief. Ready to burst, we walk away from the truck toward the little store and restaurant. We recount the story over and over to each other until we finally process the stupidity of what we have just done and how lucky we are to be alive. Both of us were raised by pacifists and are indiscriminately afraid of guns, and we are amazed by our poor judgment. Yet in Panama City, where armed guards stand on every corner and at the entrance to every store, we realize that guns in some ways just seem, if not normal, at least unavoidable.

We sail through our errand in Salamanca. The bureaucrat I speak with ascertains that yes, the Ministry of Health does have latrine supplies available. Yes, they could coordinate a delivery with their trucks and INRENARE's motorboat. No, there is no cost. Yes, there is an application process, but a simple one. All they require is a list of the households in need of supplies and the equivalent of a social security number for each head of household. We must place our order sometime next week.

To our astonishment, the chiva is waiting in La Cabima after all, so we do not have to chance hitchhiking again. I ask the driver if he can give me a few minutes to buy some groceries in the little store and he tells me he'll wait. I pick up some cheese, a few cans of tomato paste, onion, garlic, and a bell pepper. And we're on our way back to Corotú.

We drop off the pizza ingredients at Patricio's and I give him instructions for making it. Patricio and Catalina look a little dubious, but they agree to try.

"See you at lunchtime tomorrow!"

The next day, Manuel is nowhere to be found. I decide to wait so we can embark on this project together. I stop by Patricio's house at noon as he pulls four minipizzas out of the oven. Catalina gets some plates, and we sit on the front porch. Yum. They're really nicely done, and I complement Patricio on his efforts.

"Yes. They are tasty. But wouldn't they be better with some meat?"

"That's the great thing about pizza. You can put anything you want on top. You can try it with meat next time."

We lick our fingers and I ask about Manuel. Patricio and Catalina haven't seen him today either; at least they say they haven't.

The next day, still no Manuel.

With only a week before the ministry's deadline and many families scattered hither and yon, I forge ahead. Just paddling and walking to each house in the community takes a full day, to say nothing of the extra time needed for gossip, refreshments, and explaining the latrine program.

I give my spiel to each family, ending with, "The ministry has free supplies. Do you want to order some?" To my surprise, not everyone wants to. Some are suspicious about giving their names and identification numbers to a government agency. Since the community of Tranquilla does not officially exist, they worry they will be discovered and driven out. Others who decline are put off by the very prospect of digging a huge hole and constructing the latrine.

"*Mucho trabajo*" (too much work).

By the deadline, fifteen households have signed on. Some of these will lessen the workload by sharing a latrine with another family. Upon submitting the list, I am ecstatic that we will have tangible news to report at the first health committee meeting.

Saturday comes, and I have not seen Manuel in over a week. Señor Patricio assures me that the young man was spotted briefly yesterday, so tomorrow's inaugural meeting is still on. Somehow it always makes me nervous when he sounds so sure.

On Sunday, the meeting time of one o'clock comes and goes. That's hardly surprising, as things can start as many as two hours late and still be considered on time in Panamá. I repeatedly run up the hill to see if members have gathered at the community center and then slink back down to my hut again, hoping to go unnoticed. The last thing I need is to be seen desperately waiting for someone to show. Finally, I give up, switch on the radio, and start making dinner.

Shortly after, Manuel stumbles into my kitchen. Ironically, the would-be leader of Tranquilla's health committee is in the throes of a drinking binge that has lasted the better part of a week.

"Where have you been, Manuel? Where are the others?"

"*No sé* [I don't know]," he slurs. Having passed the week in a drunken stupor, Manuel neglected to invite Gabi, Lorenzo, and the others to the meeting. As I hound him for an explanation, I piece together that the other committee members are as yet unaware that there is to be a health committee at all.

"I've been out there busting my ass to hold up my end of the deal. And you've done nothing, have you? And what a disgrace you are! Alcohol abuse is one of the issues the health committee should be taking on, not modeling!"

My words do not have the intended effect on Manuel's drunken ears. He sags onto the kitchen bench, leans against a pole to keep from sliding onto the ground, and says, "What did you expect? After all, *yo soy Panameño* [I am Panamanian]. We never follow through!"

Although he means his tone to be jocular, I am saddened by the self-inflicted cultural slight. Nonetheless I am emboldened by the certainty that he will not remember anything I say. I let him have it.

"Look. We are talking about a better way of life here, a healthier community. We are not talking about my community. I am passing through, remember. Another year and I am gone. You, on the other hand, are stuck here. You have no health insurance and no resources. Are you going to do something about that or are you just going to be a victim?"

He is remorseless and does not answer the question. We sit in silence for a few seconds as his eyes cross, roll, and look around the room.

"Can I borrow the book, Maria?"

My copy of *Donde no hay doctor*, the Peace Corps–issued medical handbook, is lying on the table. I'd intended to bring this first-aid guide to our so-called meeting so I could show people the kinds of references available.

"Okay," I relent, secretly pleased he's thrown me a bone. "Let me know if you have a change of heart about the committee."

From time to time I catch Manuel studying the book intently, sitting outside the school on a ridiculously small classroom desk tipped backward against the cinder-block wall, or in the tienda between customers. It can't be easy. At least Manuel can read a little, and the book is written at a basic level.

The latrine supplies arrive, and he helps dig a hole or two here and there. Eventually, one of the children delivers the book back to me. No committee ever materializes, and we are resigned again to hoping for random visits by public-health nurses bearing expired medications, and the occasional dentist with the inevitable picture of a smiling tooth. Old and young alike will forever line up to have their rotten teeth pulled.

19

Leucaena

Edgar makes no pretense. He does not want the latrine supplies. He goes out of his way to be kind to me but is suspicious of government motives no matter the issue. The quintessential loner, Edgar abstains from working with all kinds of outside technicians. He and his wife, Luciana, have an undisclosed number of children, ranging in age from six to twenty-five.

The couple lives at the tip of an isolated peninsula, just beyond Señor Patricio's place. The peninsula is fenced off with barbed wire, a metaphor for the long-standing feud between Edgar's family and the entire rest of the village of Tranquilla. It is hard to understand the divide, given how gracious and open Edgar and Luciana are with Ethan and me. I cannot remember any visit when they have not welcomed me with a refreshment of some kind—hot coffee, a glass of lemonade, or—my favorite—*pipa* (coconut water).

Pipa is a classic tropical drink, and also the name given to its source, an immature green coconut (*Cocos nucifera*). It is enjoyed following a multi-step process: a child is sent scurrying to the top of a coconut palm tree with a machete in hand. The child hacks the pipa loose and it falls to the ground. After sliding to the base of the tree, the child retrieves the pipa, carries it back to the house, and presents an adult with the prize. The adult expertly hacks a hole on a diagonal and offers his guest the cool and refreshing beverage.

I experienced my first pipa right here at Edgar's house some months ago. After downing the liquid, revitalized by its light, sweet-sour taste, I thanked Edgar as I handed the empty shell back to him. He surprised me by setting it on the ground and whacking it open with a single swing of his machete. My imagination found the splitting of the great nut, reminiscent of a human skull, unnerving. Edgar took half and offered me the other, demonstrating how to scoop out the sweet coconut meat with a teaspoon. The fruit had the texture of custard and a taste every bit as sweet as the beverage.

After one pleasant afternoon paseando with Edgar and Luciana, I ask Gladys why they have been ostracized by Tranquilla.

"The others are not in agreement with them," she says matter-of-factly. I probe deeper and find she means that Edgar and his family are ethnic minorities, Colombian refugees of African descent. As *Evangelicos* (evangelical Christians), they are also considered religiously unacceptable by the Catholic majority (and their ethnicity means that they are rejected even by many other Evangelicos).

On what should be some of the most productive soil in the village, Edgar's shack is surrounded by a sea of paja gringa. Toward the end of the rainy season last year, I worked with him on planting a large, dense patch of *guandúl* (pigeon peas, *Cajanus cajan*). Guandúl grows rapidly and produces a creamy, peppery pea—divine with coconut rice. Edgar's guandúl was my first experiment with the use of a fast-growing, perennial crop to control paja gringa—a sun-loving plant—with shade. Edgar keeps the field reasonably clear of paja, and despite spotty germination in some places the guandúl develops nicely, taller than my own five feet, eight inches. From time to time he sends me home with a cupful of peas for my supper.

Now he seems like the perfect candidate for a new project. I am keen to introduce an even faster-growing tree by the name of *leucaena* (white lead tree, *Leucaena leucocephala*). I visit him one day to present my proposal. With me I take the packet of seeds recently acquired from the INRENARE office, probably a thousand seeds in all. With a flourish, I pour the shiny seeds onto an enamel plate. I run my fingers through their luxuriant glossiness; Edgar cannot resist and does the same.

"These trees are like magic," I pitch. "They will enrich your soil, protect your crops from the winds off the lake, and provide you with plenty of firewood right next door to your house. Think how proud you will be as the first in Tranquilla to pioneer them!"

I am impressed with my own sell-job as Edgar readily agrees that to plant leucaena would be a fine thing indeed. We will plant the trees in alternating rows, with food crops, such as corn and beans, planted between the rows of leucaena. The only difficulty lies in the inaccessibility of Edgar's compound to others in Tranquilla. For this planting to serve as a demonstration, I have to be creative. To my delight, Edgar accepts my suggestion that we plant the young leucaena seedlings on the shore so they are visible to canoe traffic from Corotú. All visitors to Tranquilla must pass by the peninsula, so it is a great location.

First, though, we need seedlings. After my disappointing experience with acacia, I research proper pretreatment procedures for leucaena seed. Like the former, germination of leucaena first requires a dipping in boiling water. I complete this step prior to the following weekend, when Ethan and I take the seeds and three hundred gray, government-issued seedling bags to Edgar's peninsula.

In the lazy heat of the afternoon, Edgar introduces us to a boy we have never seen before. "This is el Mudo [the Mute]." The name seems cruel, so we simply avoid calling him anything. Yet we are drawn to him and soon learn that he can hear perfectly well as he gesticulates in answer to our questions. One of the older girls explains that the family met el Mudo at church. "No one knows his real name," she insists.

We take el Mudo to be about twelve or thirteen years old. His hair consists of dark, close-cropped coils. His lips are full, as if to compensate for the emptiness of his voice. His whole aura is one of tenderness. The gracefulness of his communication contrasts brightly with our own halting command of the language. From time to time, to make a particular point, he pairs a gesture with a sweet murmur. The sound, though faint, is melodic and serves as a sound track to the choreography of his motions.

We work side by side, taking our time filling the bags with Edgar's rich soil. I am pleased to see that Edgar has salvaged an old cayuco to serve as a semillero for the bags. Into each bag we place three of the precious seeds and lightly cover them with soil. Watering the bags feels celebratory. We each pour a little over our own head to quell the heat.

At the end of a glorious day, we say our farewells to the group, and Edgar's son escorts us to the gate. Something on the shore catches my eye. Upon scrutiny, I see that it is a wisp of cloth fluttering atop four spindly sticks.

"What is that thing?" I ask.

"Nothing. A house," he replies.

"A house?! Whose house?"

"Nobody's. Juana's. She lives there," he says, as if everybody knew this.

I recently learned that Juana is actually Edgar's first wife, cast aside years ago for the younger Luciana. I am horrified to think of her squatting here on her ex-husband's land, a stick figure shivering in the afternoon rains and the breeze and bugs of the night. I think of her visits to my own rancho, and the irony of her concern that perhaps my roof might leak. Why doesn't Edgar build her a proper rancho?

Over the next weeks and months I visit frequently as the seedlings grow. I half hope to see El Mudo but am disappointed again and again. Each time I visit, I avoid looking at Juana's lean-to.

But at least the seedlings flourish. Leucaena can put on five to ten feet of growth per year. Insta-trees! On the day appointed to transplant the trees from their bags into the field, Edgar is nowhere to be found and has left no explanation or apology. Luciana is home but has no intention of leaving the hammock, where she lounges wearing only a short skirt and a lacy black brassiere. She complains about the heat and, with an indifferent gesture, tells me to make myself at home. On inspection I find that at least Edgar kept his word and cleared a small planting area by the lake. The timing of the planting is critical, as a certain amount of rain is needed for the trees to establish well, and the rainy season is coming to a close.

Furious with Edgar for blowing me off, and with Luciana for her laziness, I ask their youngest son and daughter if they are game to help me plant. They are. Propelled by my anger, I determine to get all the seedlings in the ground, in no small part to shame Edgar. Together, two small children and one woman will accomplish what he himself cannot be bothered to do. We work through a heavy rain and slog away until we get the last seedling in the ground, just before dark. My frustration is replaced by a sense of accomplishment and camaraderie with the kids, exhaustion notwithstanding.

The project at Edgar's is well timed. Shortly after the leucaena seedlings are transplanted, UCLA organizes a new meeting about the steep new fees INRENARE will start assessing residents of Chagres Park starting in January. If a farmer wants to clear a field for planting, the traditional farming method practiced for centuries free of charge, he must now pay $2.50 for that privilege. The new rule prohibits cutting any live tree for any purpose unless it was planted by the person cutting it down, in which case the cutter will be charged three cents per foot. Any downed wood collected for firewood or other purposes will be assessed at two cents per foot.

Never mind that INRENARE has no way to enforce the new rules. UCLA members are offended on principle, and each of them describes in detail how these fees will affect his ability to feed his family. "It's as if they want to force us out, no?" says one farmer at the end of a lengthy speech. "INRENARE knows we cannot pay this money." I hold my tongue, as I am unsure the purpose *isn't* to force them out, but that seems beside the point right now.

I say my piece after the others have spoken. "We all know this will be a challenge to meet, but we have to offer a counterproposal if INRENARE is going to take us seriously." I try to guide the discussion toward approaching INRENARE with a "plant two trees, cut one for free" proposal. Mostly, though, folks just want to complain about how unfair the new rule is. I promise to take their concerns back to INRENARE in Panama City to see whether there is any flexibility at all in the new charges.

Ethan and I set out for the INRENARE office a few days later. We wait in La Cabima for a bus into Panama City. I sit cross-legged on the pavement, eyes closed and lightly snoozing. Soft fingers flutter across my arm and shoulders. I'm startled by this hand upon me and yet I am not alarmed, so benign is the touch that my brain registers "woman, child."

I open my eyes and see it is el Mudo. His expression is pure joy on finding us here. In a hurried exchange of pleasantries as our bus arrives, we tell him we would love to see him back in Tranquilla. He runs alongside the bus a few steps after we board, waving and smiling as we depart. We never see him again.

20

Boa

Writing a letter home, I look up from time to time at Lake Alajuela. The rainy season is upon us. I shiver and reach for my sweatshirt. It is late afternoon, and I perceive a bit of color and movement: Gabi's youngest daughters in their impossibly tiny cayuco. Rarely venturing into the village center herself, Gabi often sends her girls to the little store at this time of day for a bit of cooking oil, flour, or other necessities.

A dugout like all the others, the boat is rendered unmistakable by its tiny size and bright blue paint, with paddles to match. No doubt the paint was left over from the government-issued stuff that coats the lower half of elementary school walls throughout the developing world, Tranquilla being no exception. The girls are only four and six, but so competent is their technique already that their synchronized paddling calls to mind the deft legs of a water bug, a giant water strider. A little later, they paddle back to the family compound, their errand presumably completed.

I have finished writing my letters when I notice another, larger boat, this time approaching my own landing. Given the rarity of her appearances and the errand just run by her children, I am surprised to see Gabi herself. She is out of breath when she reaches my threshold. "Maria, I came to fetch you. Adán is sick. His family needs help."

I grab my Peace Corps medical supplies in their bright red plastic briefcase. At this point the kit contains mostly aspirin and Band-Aids, hardly lifesaving supplies. Still, I find its presence as a prop reassuring. Since the failure of the health committee, neighbors still come to me for basic first aid and medical care.

Parents have even started bringing their children to me for shots, making me unpopular with the younger set. With only book-learning credentials, I botched several early attempts, most recently alienating a toddler in need of a daily penicillin injection. According to her parents, after the first two shots she whimpered, *"Maria es mi enemiga"* (Maria is my enemy), though not within my hearing.

Despite my initial reluctance to give shots and my denial that I would do so regularly, my practical side decided to seek guidance from the Peace Corps nurse on a trip into the capital city.

"Do not give shots," was his first tip. Completely convinced, I rose to leave his office. "However, if you must . . ." He drew a picture of a buttock, slicing it into quarters with his finger. Showing me in which quadrant to place the shot, he gave me an orange for practice. Although I am never at ease with the task, I find that I can at least inject the medication with minimum discomfort for my victims.

"I guess I'm better than nothing," I reassure myself as Gabi and I climb into her dugout and she pushes off the shore. She brought an extra paddle, which is a good thing. The people at the INRENARE station, where I left my own paddle for safekeeping a while back, saw fit to give it away to someone passing through. To make matters worse, they also lost the small plank that Ethan fashioned to keep the weight off the crack in the bottom of our aging cayuco. I flew into a rage upon finding how carelessly INRENARE had treated my belongings, in this case two critical pieces of transportation equipment required to do my job. I made it abundantly clear to my INRENARE counterparts that I would not be coordinating with them further until they replaced the paddle and the plank.

Gabi and I make our way toward Adán's house in an intensifying drizzle. The house is as far from the village center as one can get without quite being *en el monte*, literally, "in the sticks." Together, Adán's house, Gabi's, and that of Señor Salvador form a suburb of sorts, whereas I live "in town." All three houses are built in traditional Emberá fashion. Stilts support a tidy floor of bark from the jira palm, suspended over the mud and rubble that we earth-dwellers in town contend with.

I imagine the worst and my paddle stirs up anxiety as it pushes through the water. We pull the boat onshore at the muelle. Now in a downpour, we start up the slick, worn trail to Adán's rancho. Despite our trepidation, we hurry to the house, in part from a sense of urgency, but also to escape the rain.

First we see Adán. He sits upright in a hammock, legs straddling either side. To my relief, he looks the picture of health and grins delightedly.

"*Buenas*," begins Gabi. "But we heard you were feeling *un poco* [a little] . . . ," and her voice weakens as we both notice the limp form of an enormous dead snake.

Adán's wife, Chita, emerges from the darkness of the rancho, her face swollen and tear-smudged. She carries a newborn baby.

We look back at Adán.

"Señor, are you well?" I am relieved that Gabi maintains her composure. My Spanish crisis vocabulary is virtually nonexistent, and I can only stare mutely at the scene.

"Does it look like he's well?" scoffs Chita. "He's been acting strange lately. To the point where I swear I'm leaving this house and taking the children with me. He went out to the hills this morning and came back with this." She gestures disgustedly to the snake. "He chases us with it, wiggling it in our faces, draping it around me!" She shudders. "I won't have it!"

Adán rubs the back of his neck as he swivels his head from side to side. Until this moment, I never noticed his predatory face. His teeth are honed, angular, and sharp. He grimaces, his face flushed. He picks up the boa by its neck and begins to stroke it, almost lovingly, and draws it into the hammock with him.

"Gabi. Maria. Like Eve, my wife is a sinner. Tell my wife that this beast is a messenger. It will teach my wife her place."

"Hear what nonsense he speaks!" screeches Chita.

Adán seems plain crazy all right, but Chita's shrill protest makes it difficult to sympathize with her. Gabi and I exchange a glance. By this time it is clear that aspirin and Band-Aids are not what the situation calls for. But what to do?

Gabi turns to Adán, and in her sternest manner orders, "Get a hold of yourself, *hombre*! It's time for you to behave like a responsible parent. An adult, *pues*. Can't you see you're frightening the children? Look. Put that thing back where you found it." She nods toward the snake. "Chita and the *niños* are coming with me. Chita, grab your things. Meet us at the boat."

Although we cannot see the other children, the curtain of rain has tapered off and we hear their low whispers, shushed inside the rancho. Chita turns toward the house and barks an order. A young boy and girl emerge, heads bowed, eyes downcast. They look to be about eight or nine, although it is hard to tell. The boy hoists a bag of rice over his shoulder while the girl gathers a bundle of clothes. They follow their mother, who carries the baby.

The forlorn little group spends the night at Gabi's. The next day, Gabi's teenage son paddles them across the lake to Corotú. They escape to Panama City, where Chita says she has family.

Although I dread running into Adán so soon after his family has left him, I must visit his neighborhood a few days later. I need not have worried. The house is quiet, his cayuco gone.

Today I seek Salvadór. The oranges we planted from seed last year are finally ready for grafting, from sweet producing tops to tough disease-resistant roots. Salvadór and I agreed on this date weeks ago. To my annoyance, no one is home. The rancho seems unusually desolate. A scrap of hammock flutters in the morning breeze. Not so much as a pot, a plate, or a piece of clothing graces the house. Trash is strewn around the yard.

Salvadór's common-law wife works as a maid in Panama City. Rumor has it he only visits her when the money runs out. Granted, he habitually lives as a virtual bachelor, but the house today is even more utterly bereft than usual of domestic niceties.

I circle around back to check over the orange seedlings. They are dry, their leaves beginning to brown and curl around the edges. Thinking to water them a little to sustain them until Salvadór's return, I pick up a discarded plastic tub from the refuse in the yard. After watering, I paddle the short distance to Gabi's, still thinking of that god-awful boa. I wonder what became of it and imagine it rotting somewhere in the forest behind Adán's rancho. My thoughts turn to irritation over Salvadór's neglect of the seedlings. Maybe Gabi knows when he will return.

I find her at home but get only as far as imparting my aggravation over Salvadór's absence. She interrupts with, "Oh, Maria. He won't be back for a long, long time. He may never return." How Gabi learned the details, I'll never know. She tells the story this way:

Hearing the confrontation the day Gabi and I intervened at Adán's house, Salvadór somehow got word to Chita, met her and the children at the bus stop in Panama City, and found lodging for all of them, presumably with his wife's money.

"You mean Chita's 'family' in Panama City is Salvadór?" I am incredulous.

"*Lo mismo* [the very same]!" she confirms. "And that's not all," Gabi continues. "Adán left for the city yesterday. He wants to track them down and bring his children back to Tranquilla. The ones that were *his*," she hisses, implying of course that the baby is Salvadór's.

Adán's antics with the boa come into focus. He clearly knew of his wife's infidelity and coped the only way he knew how.

On my way to the store the following week, I spy a dugout with two young children. A grown man paddles. The boat makes its way toward Tranquilla's back-bay neighborhood. The storekeeper nods at the lake. "Looks like Adán is back with the children."

Amazing. In the labyrinth of Panama City, with its crowds and confusion, he found them. Part of me hoped he would. Another part of me thinks the children would be better off living anonymously in the city with their mother.

The rain slowly tapers off. With the onset of the dry season, Tranquilla's men head to newly cleared fields to burn them in preparation for planting corn and upland rice. Plumes of smoke are common at this time of year, hungry flames sometimes audible from the closer fires. Sparks pose a lethal threat to the tinder-dry ranchos at this time of year.

On a particularly dry, windy day, Adán heads to his own field, about an hour's walk into the hills. He tells his children he will return after dark. "I'll get the whole field cleared. We'll plant tomorrow!" The children clean up after breakfast, oblivious to the rogue ember that lands on the rancho and burrows into the palm thatching. By the time they notice the smoke, it is too late to save the house. They form a two-person brigade to rescue clothes and bedding. The flames intensify before they can save the planting seed. They stare in horror as their best hope for food in the coming year disappears.

IV

Tree (Harvest)
January–June 1993

21

Demostración

A few weeks after Adán's house burns down, I am forced to confront my imminent return to the United States. I want a project that I have more control over, and I land on the idea of a demonstration plot. These days my Spanish is greatly improved, but maybe my ideas could be conveyed more eloquently through action than words.

I have my eye on part of the same peninsula where the farmers' cooperative sowed the plantains and papayas. In fact, a choice and highly visible location remains available, on a gently sloping bank in an area with good cayuco traffic. Surely the cooperative will allow me my own tiny *parcela* (plot)?

At a UCLA meeting, I formally request permission to carve out my own parcela, about a half acre, figuring that such a small area should be manageable. As I walk to the schoolhouse where the UCLA is meeting, my INRENARE counterpart proudly approaches, carrying a beautifully carved canoe paddle in one hand and a little bench in the other.

I can count on one hand the number of times the language barrier has actually worked in my favor, and this is one of them. In my fury over INRENARE's carelessness with my personal belongings, I told them they had given away my paddle and my *banco* (bench). What Ethan and I called a banco is actually a *planco* (plank). By this time, I had already found a replacement plank and installed it in the bottom of the boat. And now we also have a bench to sit on at home. I thank my counterpart and assure him that now we are again on good terms. He seems relieved and tilts the handle of the paddle so I can see where he has inscribed my "real" name, rendered as "Merrich." We shake hands, he beams and says good-bye, and I enter the school for the meeting.

When my item comes up on the agenda, the attendees have been at it for

a few hours already. Seemingly unimpressed, they wave a hand in acknowledgment that I can do whatever I want; it makes no difference to them. They
move on to the last agenda item.

Dozens of acres on the peninsula still languish under paja mala. I have a
budding interest in the principles of forest succession and restoration. Ethan
and I have noticed *membrillo* (heaven lotus, *Gustavia superba*) and other pioneer trees sprouting up even in the densest areas of paja. If that can happen
seemingly overnight in the unlikeliest of circumstances, what would happen
if we were to facilitate it?

Such a small plot makes it possible for us to prepare the site in a much
more intensive manner than UCLA used in the plantain field, for example.
However, we recognize that we will not be here to maintain the plot indefi-
nitely. It is unlikely that anyone will tend the plot on our behalf after we
depart. To give it the best shot at being self-maintaining, we must make it
totally paja-free and create a vegetation-free barrier for protection from escaped fires, like the one that claimed Adán's rancho.

As we paddle to the plot on the first day of work, I think of my privileged
position. I can take risks that subsistence farmers cannot. If this plot fails,
my monthly stipend will continue to buy my rice and beans. Such a failure
to one of my neighbors would mean ruin.

My thoughts become daydreams and I bask in the premature satisfaction
of a job well done. My mind's eye already sees a mature forest growing on
that very spot. The trees tower over the now diminished surrounding paja,
providing natural habitat and deep shade. Ah, yes! What took us so long to
do a demonstration?

Even before we alight, the barricade of paja intimidates us. Nothing remains to be done but hack through one stem at a time. Each stalk is at least
as thick as a broomstick. We start out working side by side, but it is hard to
see through the dense stalks and foliage. A careless move could result in a
bad cut by either a machete or a sharp stalk. We decide to work far apart to
avoid the former, Ethan at the top of the hill and I at the bottom.

Evil, evil grass! Despite the leather work gloves we wear, the jagged remains of a recently sliced stalk in turn slice open Ethan's right index finger
as he reaches to untangle a bootlace. It reminds me of a scorpion we killed
the other day. We found it in the woodpile, and I quickly followed my first
instinct, which was to grab the machete and slice it in half. The front half
took a few steps and retreated back under the woodpile. The back half bus-

ied itself stinging the machete over and over again—that is, until I minced it into little bits. By rights that's what we should be doing with the paja now, but Ethan's finger needs first aid.

We abandon work for the day and go home to clean the gushing wound. We sanitize, tweeze away grit, and pinch it together with a butterfly bandage, hoping for the best. Catalina's brother-in-law recovered from his run-in with a paja stalk a few months ago. I replenished all the ointments and bandages in my medical kit on a recent run to the Peace Corps office, so Ethan's chances of avoiding infection are good.

A few days later, Ethan's finger seems to be on the mend. Back at the plot, we make slow, steady progress on clearing the planting area. Exactly four trees, all membrillos, have volunteered within the confines of the plot. We find them peeking shyly above the paja, small periscopes making their way from the murky depths for a view of the world above. We carefully clear around each one. These brave little trees are the jump-start for a future forest of sorts, a grove to memorialize our years in Tranquilla.

Once we have reduced the paja to stubble, we work on root removal. For this we use shovel and pick to uproot the bulk of the rhizomatous growth. We are as thorough as possible; even the tiniest root fragment can resprout with a vengeance.

Drive in the pick. Wedge loose the root mass. Shake off the soil. Toss aside. Repeat. Hurling the roots into the surrounding sea of paja eases the drudgery. "Take that!" we sing, delirious with heat and progress.

Then we clear a perimeter of about ten feet to serve as a firebreak and pile stalks on the far side of it, creating an additional protective barrier higher than our heads. As if to remind us of its immortality, new paja roots claw at the air around the piled stalks in our external barrier. It lives.

Occasionally I work on clearing the plot alone while Ethan is away at the Smithsonian research station. Being out here gives me a new perspective on the life of the village—who visits whom and how often, who collects firewood where, the most popular fishing spots. Most passersby do not stop, but they occasionally shout up a greeting or a piece of news. Much to my annoyance, a drunken Manuel happens by from time to time. "Maria! You work too hard! Come drink!"

"*Sí, cómo no*, Manuel!" As if.

It takes weeks, but we finally have a clean plot of black, crumbly soil. It is the most fertile in the region, an accumulation of all the topsoil that has washed downhill thanks to slash-and-burn agriculture. We see ourselves as liberators, having freed the vitality of this parcela. The result poses an astonishing contrast to the tired, weakened soils more commonly farmed.

Although the slope to the lake is gentle, with no roots or vegetation, the plot is now vulnerable to erosion and the loss of all that beautiful soil. We retrieve our small stash of *canavalia* (jack bean, *Canavalia ensiformis*) seeds. A Ministry of Agriculture extension agent gave them to me a few months ago. I have been saving the beans for just such an occasion. They are quick to sprout and are robust in full sunlight and droughty conditions. Considered "green mulch," or an edible cover crop, jack beans actually enrich and protect the soil. The leaves are good animal fodder, the beans a reasonable protein source for humans. All these qualities make them a perfect first crop to introduce to the tidy new plot.

Within parallel rows five feet apart along contours, we sow one seed every foot. We have just the right amount for the entire parcela at this spacing. We water each one for the next few days and are rewarded with a rapid, near-complete emergence within a week. The young plants look surprisingly vigorous given their tender age. My pride swells over the early success of this planting. Sometimes I go to the plot just to sit and admire them.

Each return visit to the plot is also a search-and-destroy mission for newly sprouted paja. I always bring a machete along and never fail to spend a few minutes knocking it back. My disdain for the enemy is entangled with a sense of respect. More than anything, the paja has a will to live, and in my experience it never gives up.

Finally, with the success of the jack bean planting and the paja more or less under control, we can supplement the food crops with more pioneer trees. Here is where my little tree nursery at home comes in handy.

My recent focus has been on growing trees native to Panamá. I have developed some worries over how aggressive leucaena can be, for example. For the plot, I favor *albizia* (Caribbean albizia, *Albizia niopoides*), a native pioneer species. It fixes nitrogen, grows rapidly, and is renowned as a good shade tree. Shading is essential given that it is the centerpiece of our strategy to control paja. Planting is pure joy after the seemingly endless work of clearing the paja. We interplant a few other species, such as balo, to bolster diversity.

The seedlings are still young and vulnerable but growing well. At this stage, I host a new group of Peace Corps trainees on a tour of projects around Lake Alajuela. A few UCLA members join us, too, and I finally see a flicker of understanding in their eyes. We stroll through the parcela, and I point to the trees that promise to be the best nectar producers. The UCLA has developed an interest in beekeeping recently, so its members are particularly eager to plant good trees for honey production. The parcela tethers our lofty discussions to the ground. I may never find out the ultimate fate of our little demonstration site. But I like to think we gave it the best possible chance of becoming a forested nucleus in a sea of paja.

22

Almejas

Several months have passed without further talk of witchcraft. But this morning, on my way to Edgar's to check on the leucaena seedlings, Señora Catalina tells me that he has hexed her household.

"How so?" I ask.

"By making the sign. You'll see it on your way out there."

I continue on and see it lying on the ground at the gate. A machete lies on top of a stick sharpened on both ends. Together, they form the letter *X*. I actually hesitate to step over it. After all, the last thing I need is to be hexed.

"Don't be ridiculous," I mutter to myself. I decide to pick up the machete and return it to Edgar. I'll just play innocent. As I retrieve the implement and cast the stick aside, I find myself thinking, "Honestly, Edgar. You really shouldn't run with the Devil like that. A nice guy like you." Edgar is not home, so I present the machete to his children. "Your *papá* must have left this in the path by accident."

After a few minutes of admiring the leucaena planted along the shore, we sit down and dabble idly in the water. The children point out that the lake has finally receded enough that clamming season will soon be upon us. To demonstrate, they scoop handfuls of silt. Sorting through the muck, we find a dime-sized creature that had been happily burrowed in the mud until now.

"Just wait and you'll see how great the clamming is in a few days!" they exclaim.

As a tangible acknowledgment of the park's unofficial inhabitants, the Panamanian government stocked Lake Alajuela with all kinds of edible creatures. Tilapia, for instance, a relative of piranhas, can weigh nearly ten pounds. Boys and young men in the village regularly catch smaller fish simply using a small Clorox bottle with fishing line wrapped around it. For my own fish,

I depend on kids who stop by the house occasionally, selling it for twenty-five cents a pound. Thus, I am intrigued by the possibility of clams, which I actually have a shot at gathering for myself.

Sure enough, a few days later we are well into the dry season and the lake drains rapidly to keep the Panama Canal operational. Eager for new ways to supplement my protein-poor diet, I make my way again to Edgar's house. The two youngest kids say the best way to get at the clamming hot spots is by boat. We push off and are soon scooping handfuls of mud and plucking out nickel-sized clams to toss into a bucket of clean water. We come away with a pailful and divide them, and I happily head home to get them cleaned up for supper.

As instructed, I rinse the clams more thoroughly at home. Then I build a fire and set a large pot of water on to boil. As the steam twists toward the roof, I pop the clams in and watch in fascination as the shells pull apart, all vestiges of my former vegetarianism by now evaporated. I drain the water and allow the clams to cool. Extracting the tiny pads of flesh from each pair of shells is painstaking but gratifying work. After thirty minutes, I have a full cup of clams. When Ethan returns from his volunteer job that evening, we enjoy pasta in a sauce of sautéed clams and garlic. The clams are lake-flavored, chewy morsels. I have never had them so fresh.

I quickly notice that our culinary adventure in chowders, soups, and stews is not of interest to our neighbors. Clams are not a traditional part of the campesino diet. With few options for supplementing their subsistence economy with real dollars to purchase medications and other necessities, they value the clams more as income than as protein. So, they are sold to fancy hotels in Panama City that serve wealthy tourists.

Of all things, clams also serve to unite the Catholic and Protestant factions of the community. When I first moved to Tranquilla, I learned of the divide between the majority Catholics and the minority Evangelicos. Catholicism is the government-sponsored religion, the default for anyone who doesn't want to give it a lot of thought. "I'm not a religious person," I sometimes hear people say, "but I'm Catholic." The Catholics see all Protestants as religious fanatics. The rift has proven deeper and wider than I ever imagined. There are precisely two things, though, around which all of Tranquilla rallies. The school is one, and clams are the other.

Men of all religious persuasions team up in their boats to haul clams from the lake. Women gather at each other's houses each day to shuck the clams on a huge scale. They sit on benches surrounding a large fire on which a cauldron boils away to open the clams, much as I did in my own tiny kitchen. After the clams are shucked, the men take them into the city to sell to the fancy restaurants and hotels and split the profits of their combined labor.

Elated over our new discovery, I decide to pour heart and soul into clamming season. I ask around and find out the group will gather at Señor Lorenzo's house the following day. The next morning, I trot over to lend a hand just for the joy and camaraderie of the experience. I am smug with the certainty that I have finally picked up the rhythm of the community. Together we will work, sit around, chat, and tell jokes. I might even go home with a small handful of rubbery clams for tonight's soup.

As I approach the house, I see a half dozen women already chattering and working away. The scene is festive and playful. Then one of them spots me, and a hush descends on the group. The silence continues as I near them, and no one offers me a seat or makes room for me on the benches around the fire. They offer only a scattered, stony *"Buenas"* in response to my greeting. Thus shunned, I try to think of what to do next. I have lived here eighteen months, and my sense of belonging, though not complete, makes me feel entitled to a better welcome than this. To save face, I shuck a few token handfuls of clams, contribute them to the community pot, and make my excuses.

I depart fuming, my feelings badly hurt as I go home to sulk. I turn on the radio, write a few letters home, and straighten things around the house feeling pretty sorry for myself.

Edgar's oldest son saw the whole thing happen. At dinnertime, he arrives at my house with a string of fish. I try to pay him, but he refuses. "No, no, Maria. I got them for you." He leaves me to have my dinner in peace. I think he recognized my marginalization for what it was. After all, as an Evangelico, he experiences discrimination on a daily basis. If he was trying to cheer me up, or even if he wasn't, it worked.

When I am able to think coherently again, I wonder what on earth the problem was. Clearly this was women's work, so for once I did not overstep gender boundaries. Then it dawns on me. I realize that, precisely because the clams are strictly a cash crop, the women worried that I would want a cut of the profits they were counting on for themselves. I did not make my intentions clear upon arrival. Soured on the experience, I am not about to go back and try to explain so I can join in the fun tomorrow or the next day. Instead, I vow to stick to harvesting occasional clams for personal use only.

23
Quinceañera

As Gabi's youngest child is still in the making, her oldest daughter, Ana, is turning fifteen and we are celebrating. We bustle around Gabi's kitchen in about as close to a frenzy as one ever gets in Panamá's countryside. I still glow from the honor of Gabi asking me to help host the quinceañera (sweet fifteen celebration).

Somehow, streamers and balloons materialize and we blow ourselves giddy. Gabi tends to each small child swarming underfoot in need of *chibui* (cheese curls), a trip to the latrine, or a nap. I have not yet seen Ana, who has spent all morning in the house primping. I whisk through my assignment of sweeping the earthen floor free of chicken droppings and other debris.

As the sun sets, we settle down, resting before the guests trickle in after dark. Gabi spoons a stew from the kettle into my bowl, then some for each child, and finally serves herself. We are all fed and the dishes washed before the party begins.

Gabi asks me to prepare *palomitos de maíz* (little doves of corn), a fitting name for popcorn. Because I have taught myself to produce fluffy batches over a wood fire, introducing palomitos to Tranquilla may be my biggest achievement as a Peace Corp Volunteer. I pop several batches. The aroma, warm and rich, provides a focal point for the festivities. Gabi's children form a semicircle around me and beg for just a taste. We spoon it into large plastic shopping bags for serving.

Two rustic wooden planks are transformed by plastic party tablecloths into a refreshment table. Gabi and I line up the food. First the popcorn. Then, loose bags of cheese curls, and stacks of golden hojaldres. The cake, however,

is the centerpiece. Gabi fetched it from La Cabima today. Draped in gaudy
mounds of blue, green, and pink frosting, the cake rules the refreshment table.
It demands the attention of all partygoers with its cheery message, "Happy
birthday Gabriela." Gabriela? I look up at Gabi with raised eyebrows, and she
explains that the bakery copied her name from the order, not understanding
that it was actually for Ana. The cake is nonetheless a hit. Few of the guests
can read, and those who can find it funny.

Gabi's husband tests the strength of a special batch of *chicha fuerte* (corn
liquor), which he began fermenting two weeks prior, especially for the occasion. For women and children, Gabi provides *chicha de nance*, my favorite
nonalcoholic alternative.

Ethan is the first among the guests to arrive and I take this as my signal
to scurry to the shower for some privacy to change into my party clothes—a
madras skirt, collared blouse, and sandals. I am always nervous about wearing open shoes at night when snakes are not visible, but I make an exception
today. I'll step back into my boots before we make the trip home.

Gabi calls up to Ana to stop primping and come greet her first guests. Ana
is demure in a flouncy top and ruffled skirt cut just above the knee. A head-
band twists around her shoulder-length curls and her smile is shy and self-
conscious. She slips into plastic jellies, like Cinderella's glass slippers, as her
mother swoons, "There. You are so *bonita* [pretty], Ana. I was going to surprise you with this later, but here is your gift now. It is perfect with your outfit."

Pulling a slender box from her pocket, Gabi prods Ana to open it. She does
so and gasps. Usually undemonstrative, Ana is stunned by her mother's gift.

"Maria, put it on her. My hands are too trembly."

Such an intimate gesture, and I hardly know Ana. Still, she permits me
as her mother's friend, though I am closer to Ana's age than to Gabi's. I fas-
ten the clasp of the gold-plated chain behind her fifteen-year-old neck. The
A glitters in the lamplight.

Ana's older brother has lent his radio for the occasion and Gabi tunes it
to Radio Mia for traditional Panamanian folk music. In addition to the cake
and decorations, she has a fresh supply of batteries to keep the music going.
Gabi is a born organizer.

As guests arrive, they drift into the shadows of the rancho, where they
shrink together on benches until the festivities are officially underway. When
a critical mass is finally there, Gabi nudges her husband, Augusto, to make a
fatherly announcement. He begins in his shy way, staring intently at a spot on

the floor. "Tonight, we celebrate the coming-of-age of our firstborn daughter." He clears his throat a couple of times and continues, "We thank you for coming to our celebration in her honor."

Sensing that Augusto is about done with his remarks, Gabi breaks in, "And we hope you'll share in the fun with us and enjoy a little *chicha fuerte*. But at the first sign of drunkenness or disrespectful behavior, I'll throw you right out on your ass. This is a celebration of womanhood, nothing more." Augusto continues to stare at the floor, probably wishing it would swallow him whole.

With the conclusion of Gabi's dubious welcome, the dancing begins. The staid movement is not so different from other gatherings in the village, but I enjoy it many times more in my unfamiliar role as a cohostess. I join Gabi in circulating with chicha and palomitas, encouraging guests to visit the refreshment table. I dance with little kids and with Ethan. The young men of Tranquilla are never so bold as to ask me to dance, even when Ethan is not in town. After a while, I rest with Ethan on a bench in the shadows, watching the dancers.

Augusto strides over and slips a cup into my hand. Ethan has already been steadily drinking his chicha, and it turns out that I have just been given the hard stuff also. Perhaps I am being tested to see if I will set it aside as a true lady. The truth is that I am curious, so I immediately sip at the vile, lumpy stuff. It reminds me of my mother's crock of brandied fruit. She used to keep it in our pantry, restoking it from time to time. Not eager for a refill, I sip at the portion I have, internally rejoicing at this gesture from Augusto.

Finally, it is time to cut the cake. Gabi leads everyone in a feeble round of "*Cumpleaños feliz*" (Happy Birthday). She then coaxes Ethan and me into singing the song in English, so we belt it out together, a big hit. "Make a wish, Ana! What do you want for your *quinceañera*?" "*Un gringo*," she jokes.

"Not mine!" I retort, to much laughter.

24

Lorena

Gabi and I are now easy together, in and out of each other's ranchos a few times a week. Today, she praises my beloved *lorena* stove and wonders if she might be able to have one herself.

Outwardly, I calmly agree to help if Augusto will provide the needed sand from the river and clay from the banks of the lake. Inwardly, I dance a jig in celebration of my first lorena customer in the village. A Peace Corps Volunteer from a nearby village trained me in the basics of lorena stovecraft. The word *lorena* is a compilation of two Spanish words: *lodo* (mud) and *arena* (sand). The first lorena I built was under the tutelage of my colleague. I apprenticed myself to another lorena team shortly thereafter and have been itching to apply the clever concept in Tranquilla ever since.

Most households in Tranquilla still prepare meals on open fires, in a single large pot supported on three stones. One threat to the forests of the Panama Canal watershed is the gathering of wood for cooking fires. In theory, lorena stoves double the efficiency of firewood, thus lessening the pressure on the forest ecosystem, one of the Peace Corps's main goals.

After Augusto has acquired all the materials, Ethan and I lay a large sheet of corrugated metal on the ground. We use shovels to mix the dried sand and clay together and add a few handfuls of rice hulls to provide a hint of structure for binding. We finish the mixing with our bare hands, encouraging small pockets of pure clay and sand to mingle together.

Sprinkling in a tiny amount of water, we run our fingers through the pile to moisten the ingredients. Then, a little more water and mixing. We finally achieve the perfect consistency, but I continue to fondle it longer than necessary. The cool graininess soothes a nagging itch between my fingers, the result of a tenacious fungal infection that has plagued me over the last several months.

When properly moistened, a good lorena mixture is like pie dough. The mix should be just barely moist enough to hold together when squeezed. With pie dough, the concern is that too much liquid will cause the pastry to become gummy, ruining the crust's flaky integrity. With a lorena, excess moisture results in deep cracks and a weakened structure.

Augusto has built a solid base on which we construct the stove. Ana smacks the first scoopful of stove mix onto the base. Gabi follows, then Ethan and I. We pound and prod each layer with our fists and then use a heavy *pilón* (large wooden pestle). The objective is to create a dense brick that will later be carved to form the inner workings of the stove. With each thrust of the pilón, we eliminate microscopic air pockets. This is the hardest part, so we take turns. As we work, a natural alchemy transforms the humble ingredients from a shapeless pile into a coherent mass about one-fifth the volume of the raw materials.

The result is impressive. We admire the sheer size of the block, its smoothed elegance and chocolate hues. Our work for the day complete, we must allow the block to settle and cure for several days before carving.

When we return home, it is already dark. Ethan lights the kerosene lamp, and I light the fire in the burn chamber of our own lorena. As I set water on to boil for pasta, I try to shake off a low-level anxiety. I have helped make other stoves, but Gabi's is the biggest I have attempted. There is also a lot riding on this first stove for Tranquilla. Whether others become interested in having their own will depend on how much Gabi likes hers. It feels like Gabi is giving me a chance to show my stuff, and I hope not to disappoint.

A few days later, we begin the carving phase. Thoughts of mud pies and pastry dough are cast aside as we enter the realm of sculpture and masonry. Today we use only the simplest of tools—kitchen spoons.

Gabi has created her own design, describing it to us as we sketched it out. Now we implement her vision, starting with a large firebox to accommodate sizable fuel; a far cry from the diminutive sticks we use at home in our smaller stove. A wide, short tunnel will shunt heat and flame to the next burner. Gabi wants intense heat for both burners, so she can boil and fry at the same time. A second tunnel will connect to a third "burner," set above the others. This one will be for simmering, or to keep her husband's dinner warm. "When he is delayed in the fields," she explains.

Finally, a longer tunnel will transport the dregs of combustion into the chimney, fashioned of corrugated metal with wire fasteners. The tall chimney will exhale smoke and cinders through the ceiling, into the roof's penca. Gabi's eyes will thus be protected from the smoke, which instead can be focused on repelling pests that live in the thatch.

We carve chambers and tunnels. Like miners, we simultaneously create and explore the depths of the stove. With our spoons, the four of us scrape, caress, mold, and smooth. Ethan leads the charge, with an industrial kitchen–sized stirring spoon, punching the holes that get us started. Gabi and I follow, each burrowing and sculpting with aluminum serving and soup spoons. These occasionally bend or break, and I make a mental note to buy replacements on my next trip to the city. Ana follows behind with a teaspoon, using the back of it to smooth the tunnel walls and the exterior of the stove. My respect for spoons heightens. I jokingly vow never again to take these versatile tools for granted.

As I hear myself extolling the virtues of the common spoon, I feel a sense of guilty pleasure. Then my mind ushers forth a memory of using spoons in just such a way. When I was nine, my parents were horrified to find that my friends and I had been amusing ourselves by digging "caves" in the foundation of our stately brick house in Atlanta. The basement was nothing more than an incongruous hole in the ground, our foundation "unfinished" Georgia red clay. Where we saw cozy homes for our dolls and stuffed animals, my parents could think only of the house caving in. Now I am a grown-up Peace Corps Volunteer who practically has orders to dig holes with a spoon. What could be better?

In comparison with the tunnels, burners are intuitive and easily conjured. One simply scratches a sketch around the outer diameter of the largest pot one anticipates using on that burner. The resulting circle angles inward, thus enabling a sturdy nesting of smaller pots and skillets as desired.

Tunnels, in contrast, are a leap of faith. Connecting firebox to burners to chimney, they must somehow add up to the functioning system that is the stove. Heat rises, and the tunnel floor must in turn rise, ramp-like, from the beginning to the end of the fire's journey. As a system, the tunnels must be deep enough within the stove that the structure is maintained, avoiding collapse under heavy pots. Tunnels must be just the right diameter to transport heat but not allow it to pass through too quickly. With a robust fire, our three-burner model facilitates the passage of flame from firebox to burner, a real boon.

Finally, our system is complete. Gabi will continue cooking on her open fire for the next two weeks as the stove cures. Lighting a fire in the stove too soon could mean one of two things: either a disappearing fizzle or disastrous cracking as moisture deep within the clay looks for an escape route. The first fire is always small and cool, lit only to complete the drying process, not to cook a meal.

The timing is good. I have plenty to distract me with Peace Corps training and workshops in Panamá's Interior. Ethan will be busy volunteering at the Smithsonian Research Institute. We will reconvene for the inaugural fire later.

Weeks later, upon our return to Tranquilla, Ethan and I unpack our bags. As we settle in and put the rancho in order, Gabi's two youngest daughters shyly approach us. "*Mi mamá* says, 'come here,'" lisps the older of the two.

We follow the girls in our own boat and on arriving find Gabi frying tortillas in a big pan over the firebox. A pot of hot water for tea sits on the second burner. The third holds a plate of finished tortillas, kept warm. She grins when she sees us and triumphantly flips a tortilla onto a plate, which she hands to us. "Try this."

These are no run-of-the-mill tortillas! As we savor their brilliant sweetness, she tells us they are made with *maíz nuevo* (fresh corn), rather than the typical dried meal. She explains she was too excited to wait for us and has been cooking meals on the stove since last night's dinner. I am elated, but on closer inspection I notice a single deep crack through which some smoke escapes. The defect slightly mars my pleasure over Gabi's triumph.

Soon, we notice in a corner of the kitchen a miniature stove made from leftover materials. Gabi cannot conceal her pride as she points out its salient features. A two-burner, the stove is even outfitted with a tiny chimney. Quite possibly, we are looking upon the world's first "Easy-Bake" lorena stove.

"The girls will have to learn to cook eventually, right? I figured I would try this all by myself and surprise you. So you can see how it turned out, *así, más o menos* [like the big one, more or less] . . ." She trails off modestly.

Whether the tiny stove ends up working or not, for me it is a powerful symbol that Gabi feels the lorena is worthy of emulation. As her girls pretend to cook on it, will they take in the conservation purpose, the original inspiration for the project? Probably not, but it may reinforce the value of trying new ways of doing things. And that, after all, is what we are after.

25
Miel

I am faint with panic, although we stand a full fifty feet from the hives. My phobia is bad enough around docile species, such as the European honeybee (*Apis mellifera*). Today, we face the stuff of horror films, "killer bees" (*Apis mellifera scutellata*), an aggressive hybrid famous for attacking en masse. I am embarking on a new project—beekeeping for subsistence farmers. The bees we will keep are the Africanized "killers" that have flourished in Panamá ever since they invaded the country in the 1980s.

Unfortunately, the Ministry of Agriculture has assigned Jorge, the same letch who came on to me during Natural Resources Month, to our project. He briefs us on bee biology. Although he is twice my age, he has persisted in propositioning me throughout our acquaintance. Now, squat and pot-bellied, he slicks back his thinning black hair. His tiny mustache glistens as he delivers a salacious lecture on the mating responsibilities of drone bees. Jorge describes a harem-based fantasy in which he plays the leading role. He points his sweaty lips in my direction several times during this monologue, and a few of the farmers chuckle. I clench my fists in irritation but doubt he notices. Can we just get on with the beekeeping, please?

We suit up on the fringes of the apiary, like doctors preparing for surgery. We don coveralls made of thick white cotton, pull on elbow-length leather gloves, and stretch white veils over our hats. Tucking the head net around my collar, I am thankful for the protection from stingers and also for the additional barrier between Jorge and me. I swelter in the folds of the oversized suit and force myself toward the hives.

Jorge begins the demonstration. He holds a smoker, an old-fashioned accordion-like contraption. He collects a wad of *hierba* (green grass), and places it in the combustion chamber. He lights it with a match and closes the top. The *hierba* smolders, yielding a sweet, cool smoke, which has a sedating effect on the bees and calms me also.

Pumping the smoker, Jorge dribbles its vapor across the top of the first hive and opens the lid. The aroma deepens, and my anxiety returns. A thousand tiny wings beat in anger as the throng coalesces into assault formation. They disperse and hurtle toward us. As they distribute scattershot across the coveralls of my compadres, I perceive insistent little pelts on my shoulders, back, arms, and legs. I thrill to a sense of imperviousness and lean over to look into the hive. My back arches as several sharp stings pierce my suit where it stretches tight at the hip. Against Jorge's advice, my hand instinctively swats at the assailants and I consider bolting.

Jorge maintains his composure and applies more smoke. I begrudgingly admire his grace and calm as he speaks quietly to the bees. "*Calmense, mis abejitas. Así. Así. Tranquilas, señoras mías*" (Calm yourselves, my little bees. There, there. Be tranquil, my ladies). They settle into a smoke-induced stupor, and Jorge lifts out a frame to examine. A cluster of confused bees hangs beard-like from the frame's bottom, and Jorge uses a soft brush to wipe them gently back into the hive.

What brings Jorge and me together with these foreign killer bees is our shared hope that they will become a joint vehicle for conservation and income in poor rural villages of Panamá. In this year of 1992, a single liter of honey fetches five dollars at the market, a full day's wage for a campesino farmer. Planting and conserving nectar-producing trees could replace some of the slash-and-burn agriculture that has become widely unsustainable in this region. Visions of the blessings of bees can take hold of the imagination. The UCLA is off to a promising start.

But soon, the beekeeping languishes in the countryside and Jorge struggles to keep projects going in a dozen remote villages. A fear of failure at my own responsibilities for developing Tranquilla's economy finally trumps my aversion to bees—and to Jorge.

I confront Jorge at his office. A friend accompanies me, to discourage his verbal groping. I lay out my concerns. Jorge strokes his chin as if considering the matter and delivers a string of vulgarity regarding the liberal morals of gringas. I gape at him across the piles of paper on his desk and exchange glances with my friend. We rise to leave.

Jorge follows us out, saying, "We need equipment, then. A workshop with real training. You and I could spend a lot of time together that way, Maria." He draws closer. "But where will we find the money?" All melodrama, palms outstretched, he casts his eyes toward the sky.

A few weeks later, while browsing in the Peace Corps office library, I pick up a brochure for the Farmer to Farmer program sponsored by the US Agency for International Development. The program sends volunteer agricultural experts, including beekeepers, to developing nations in a technical exchange with local experts.

I am reluctant to involve Jorge, but Tranquilla and its neighboring villages cannot qualify for the program without a local beekeeping contact. I fill out the application and drop a copy by his office. He winks at me and grins as if he knew I would come around. I recoil and hustle to the bus stop.

At last, one day the fax machine at the Peace Corps office spits out a congratulatory message from Farmer to Farmer. The program will cover all expenses for a five-day workshop. Equipment costs for several communities will also be covered. Best of all, a professor of apiculture from the extension service at Penn State will assist with the workshop and field training for a two full weeks.

I greet Professor Russell Ewert at the airport. "Call me 'Buzz,'" he smiles delightedly. "Everyone else does." I learn that he loves Panamá and visits at every opportunity. He is fresh from springtime in Pennsylvania, and his bespectacled face is already flushed with the Panamanian heat. He admits to knowing *muy poco* (very little) Spanish. Privately, I think this shortcoming could be an advantage, as he will be oblivious to Jorge's obscenities. I smile politely and tell him I would be happy to translate.

During the first days of his visit, we work our way around several communities, examining a handful of hives in each. I spend much of the week sandwiched between the two men, translating for Jorge what Buzz cannot communicate by demonstration alone. Despite our constant proximity, Jorge is caught up in an exchange of expertise with his North American counterpart and temporarily forgets to harangue me.

Buzz learns firsthand the challenges each community faces. In San Juan de Pequañi the hives are unproductive. In Tranquilla, overcrowding is an issue. Two of the Quebrada Benitez hives have been abandoned, their colonies vacating their quarters likely due to overcrowding. We peer inside each box, Buzz produces a diagnosis, and I translate.

Our workshop is scheduled to begin Monday morning, and I am apprehensive. The official start time of nine o'clock comes and goes without the appearance of instructors or participants at the schoolhouse. We invited five from each community, trusting the rural grapevine to pass the word. Around ten o'clock, a motorboat approaches. Thank God!

Jorge and Buzz arrive together. Then the cooks for the workshop, three of Tranquilla's matrons, saunter into the school's kitchen, where they find twenty-five pounds of rice and fifteen pounds of beans, delivered as promised by Jorge himself. Five young men from Victoriano Lorenzo appear. Participants trickle in until I realize that, including the five from Tranquilla, we are oversubscribed by two. All are young men. Not surprising, but I had hoped there might be one or two women.

Jorge lectures on the first morning. Buzz, whom Jorge still deferentially calls "Doctor Ewert," provides a little input mostly in the form of charades, to the bewildered amusement of the workshop participants. Jorge asks the young farmers to imagine their lives transformed by the stream of miracle products generated by their hives. In addition to the honey, there are candles to be produced from the wax. Bee pollen is considered by some to be the most nutritious food on earth.

"And as for the magical properties of royal jelly? Well let's just say that gringos will pay more than twenty dollars for a tiny bottle."

Exaggerating the economic benefits of beekeeping seems to me a terrible idea, but I hold my tongue. I ache to get outside, uninspired by the drab little schoolroom. We bake under the metal roof, the honeycombed openings in the cement-block walls providing only the tiniest bit of air circulation. Maybe this is how those bees feel right before they swarm.

I rejoice that the rest of the workshop is hands-on, with two days of demonstration and application, including *robando la miel* (robbing the honey). *Miel*, the Spanish word for honey, is an utterance of sticky sweetness. More than a name, it connotes both taste and feel in the speaker's throat.

Our group of thirty-one travels among the poorest lakeshore communities in UCLA's now not-so-new dugout canoe fitted with the outboard motor from its old boat. In each village, we remove honey-laden frames from the hives and replace them with empties. On day four we set up shop in Tranquilla's Catholic church, the only building clean enough for bottling. The surroundings underscore the sanctity of our work.

A local youth drags a knife blade across the first frame, removing the caps that adorn each hexagonal cell. He uncovers each side with reverence before placing the frame gently in the extractor. "Extractor" seems too fancy a term for this convivial fifty-five-gallon barrel with a reeled handle. We watch with satisfaction as the young man cranks. The action flings the honey at the sides of the barrel, its sweetness filling the sanctuary.

The sides of the barrel are soon honey-coated. The honey pools at the bottom, where a spigot is rigged for dispensing into bottles. I pick up one of the glass containers and hold it to the light streaming through the open doors of the church.

The workshop has been an unqualified success. Jorge calls for a round of applause for the visiting gringo "doctor of beekeeping." Buzz flushes with pleasure. With great effort, in his own Spanish, he stammers his encouragement for the project to everyone's bafflement. "Hard work better, these also surely killer bees save village." As he stumbles through some closing remarks about the bright future of "rainforest honey," a stray bee alights on my shoulder. She still appears to be doped up and probably poses no threat. Still, I shudder and reflexively brush her off. Through my phobias, I now see the utility of killer bees and lewd technicians. Still, I can only bring the respect into focus at arm's length.

26

Bosque

With only a few months remaining in Panamá, I suddenly feel nostalgic. Ethan and I are on our way to the home of Señor Oscar, our most distant neighbor. Oscar and his wife are Tranquilla's most talented artisans, specializing in weaving sombreros and fine baskets. I am eager to requisition one of each before leaving this place. The couple also supported the palm propagation project early on. I want to visit their young nursery of palms and see how it is growing.

We paddle to the farthest point on the shore across from el Gringo's. After securing the cayuco at the landing, we hear a "sheering" call. We are a few steps up the path when a great white bird swoops down not more than twenty feet in front of us. It's a hawk, almost completely white with only a few accents of black on its tail and wings. Without once touching the ground, it grasps a thick snake in its talons and within seconds rests comfortably on the lower branch of a tree next to the path. Entranced, we want to watch the bird devour its writhing meal. But something frightens the hawk, and it flies off, clinging tenaciously to its prey, which has grown limp and still.

We travel through an area of lush regrowth in an old clearing. A colony of oropendolas has moved in, a few dozen nests hanging like scattered Christmas stockings throughout the opening. I close my eyes and for a moment I am convinced I can actually hear the rustle of the jungle growing.

My trance is disrupted upon smelling an earthy smoke. We round a corner and recoil. Charred stumps litter the hillside and blackened earth stretches as far as we can see. I sink to the ground and take in the destruction. Amid the rubble of the forest, we see glimmers of life, young sprouts of yuca, corn, and rice on the hillside sloping away from the path. I feel physically ill. Two years ago, this scene would have filled me with rage. But today, how can I be angry at a subsistence farmer's attempts to feed his family?

I search for someone to blame, however, and settle on the *guardabosque* (park guard), who legitimizes these practices by writing permits for forest clearing to plant crops. The permits, two dollars apiece, are supposed to be the exception, not the rule. Yet he seems to issue them daily to people like Oscar. The guardabosque is never seen out of uniform, complete with a hat that brings to mind Deputy Dog. He wears a thick, gold-plated serpentine bracelet at all times, and a gold cross peeks out from his masses of chest hair. His lips give the impression that they are on their way to a crafty smile, which I chalk up to the regular bribes he receives, and his knowledge that more are coming. He never looks me in the eye and instead looks off to the side. I begin to wonder if he is vision-impaired.

Once we have processed the shock, we continue over the short distance to Señor Oscar's and manage a perfectly civil visit with him. He asks if we have seen his new finca. We reply that yes, it looks like the corn and yuca are coming along nicely. Oscar guides us along a path by a small creek, and we come to a spot where he has cleared much of the undergrowth. He is nursing along dozens of rare palms. Our two years have been full of cases like this—the left hand cutting down the forest, the right hand replanting it. Are we really making a difference when all is added together?

The following day, speak of the devil, who should arrive at my doorstep but the guardabosque himself. He delivers a series of pleasantries and then makes an announcement.

"We are beginning a tree registration program."

"Come again?"

"We will register the trees planted inside the park by all residents. You will help me set up visits with each family to document their plantings."

"And the purpose of the registration?" I am suspicious and probe further.

To give him credit, the guardabosque is scrupulously patient with me, taking time to ensure I understand the procedure. From what I can tell, he will arrive next week with a separate form for each household. Together, we will record the number and type of trees planted by each. To support reforestation across the nation, the Panamanian government is offering an incentive to communities like Tranquilla. Any tree they plant, whether for fruit, firewood, timber, or shade, becomes their personal property. In Chagres National Park, campesinos have no legal claim on their houses, animals, or crops. The government can confiscate any of these on a whim. Planted trees, though, will benefit their owners in perpetuity. This incentive was documented in Law 24 on November 23, 1992, and is now being implemented by INRENARE.

But there is a catch. Each person must register the trees he has planted with the local guardabosque to claim ownership. Without it, he has no proof. The guardabosque is visibly excited about the potential of the new law for the well-being of both park residents and reforestation in general. After all, he lives here too and has a family to support. I cannot help but be moved by his enthusiasm and start thinking more kindly toward him. Perhaps I have misjudged him. I agree to help.

I do my best to convey the program to Tranquilla's residents, going door to door over the next several days. My explanations go something like this: "So, you and your family live in the park. And you're not supposed to be here. This is why, no matter how many decades you remain, you will never be landowners. You will never own even the land your house is built on. Not even the finca that feeds your family. What is the next best thing, then?" Shortly after posing the question, I provide the answer.

"It is owning the trees. The very trees themselves."

As he promised, the guardabosque arrives in Tranquilla the following week to do an accounting of the trees. It's weird. Although there is something about a tree that seems wholly unpossessable, here we are listing them as possessions. Still, with pride I tally up the menagerie of trees I have had a hand in planting. Together they add up to an odd sort of forest, but a forest nonetheless. Like a pop-up book, the motley woods leap from the moldering paper of each registration form. The gmelina planted by the children mingle with Edgar's leucaena. The handful of oranges on Pablo's hillside mix it up with UCLA's papayas and plantains. Bees from Tranquilla's apiary drop by the demonstration plot, where they pollinate balo and albizia. They stream across the lake, where Navarro's acacia trees, so painstakingly grown by Señor Lorenzo, flourish. The variety, the many uses, and the numerous hands involved in their planting give a tangible sense of bounty and accomplishment.

As we visit each family to check them off, it is clear they share the pride in this menagerie. On the one hand, we are just filling out a bunch of forms stacked on a clipboard, a strictly bureaucratic endeavor. But with the stroke of a pen, each family now holds title to the first property it has ever owned.

It is likely that more forest has been lost than gained during my two years here. Still, it is clear that this ceremony of sorts has some meaning to the proud new owners. The trees are important enough to actively document and file with the government, but they can act as both carrot and stick. If the people cut down an unregistered tree, they can be fined not just for the current value of the tree but also for its future value. The threat is symbolic and unlikely to be enforced, but nagging.

So, through a conservation program comes rootedness for a people otherwise lacking any legal claim to their land. With that rootedness may come a sustainable harvest of honey, hats, firewood, fruit, beans—for both human and natural communities. And with that harvest, maybe Tranquilla will remember the gringa's peculiar ideas and ways.

27

Despedida

After summer break, school is back in session and the community seems increasingly aware that Ethan and I will be moving on. They are not an overly sentimental bunch; their primary acknowledgment of our departure comes in the form of an increased number of requests for our personal possessions. Dishes, pots and pans, furniture, the radio—all must find new homes. No one is shy about explaining why he or she should be the recipient of this or that item.

In anticipation of my close-of-service, the Peace Corps cohosts a meeting in Tranquilla with residents along with Román Diego and a few other INRENARE representatives. The purpose of the meeting is to decide whether Tranquilla will receive another Peace Corps Volunteer.

To my great embarrassment, few people attend the meeting. In fact, a couple of hours after the supposed start time, we have only ten attendees, and those only after I go door to door, beseeching residents to attend. Sensing my humiliation, Justin gently reminds me that Tranquilla has been one of the toughest communities in which Peace Corps Panama has worked during the past few years. It has admittedly been difficult to rally people to the cause of conservation and reforestation when food security is their number one issue, followed closely by adequate health care. Nonetheless, the poor attendance feels to me like a vote of no confidence.

At first, no one steps forward to offer an opinion as to the future of the Peace Corps in the community. Señor Patricio breaks the silence with, "Maria is okay, no? And she works hard. But what we really need in this community, in this park, pues, is a health or maybe agriculture Volunteer. This tree business, I mean, look around you. Trees are everywhere in Tranquilla!"

The nods and murmurs of assent are a terrible blow to my ego and some-how make the modest successes over the last two years seem wholly irrelevant. If there is no continuity for the forestry projects underway, few if any will persist. I weakly make the case once again that the long-term sustainability of the community depends on a healthy, forested watershed, but I quickly abandon the argument as I realize how defensive I sound. Moreover, if our work together over the last two years has not been persuasive enough, I am not going to convince them today. I become resigned to the idea that the only productive role I can play at this point is to support the community's desire for a new Volunteer with health or agricultural expertise and to work with Justin on making it happen.

One day I talk with Gladys at the school about finding homes for the rest of the seedlings from my personal nursery. The experiments over the past two years with germinating and growing dozens of tree varieties for all dif-ferent purposes—food, firewood, shelter, shade, crafts—have left me with a number of stragglers that now need homes. We decide to send a few soon-to-be-orphaned seedlings home with each pupil.

"And what about the *despedida*, Maria?" The farewell party. The term suits. It sounds like a diminutive form of "desperate," and that is how I am feeling right now. After the dismal outcome of last week's meeting, I figured I would just quietly pack my things, wave good-bye to whomever I happened to pass on the way out, and hitch a final ride to the chiva stop.

Noting my surprised expression, Gladys continues, as if to clarify. "The Padres de la Escuela [Parents of the School] want to celebrate the time you have spent with us. Before you leave, that is."

I am moved. Notwithstanding the lack of support for the forestry program, the community still wants to honor me—as a human being.

"The *despedida*, Maria. When should we have it?" Gladys asks again.

We agree on a date two weeks out. By Tranquilla standards, it will be a gala affair held at the school. Sadly, Ethan will be unable to attend the party, given his responsibilities at the Smithsonian Research Institute. He makes the rounds, saying good-bye to those we are closest to—Patricio, Edgar and Luciana, Lorenzo, and of course Gabi and Augusto.

On the evening of the celebration, we start in the schoolroom, and an ar-ray of children perform songs and recite poems—yes, complete with mimi-cos. We adjourn to arroz con pollo and *ensalada de feria* (festival salad). The latter is a potato salad tinted pink with the judicious addition of beets. With mayonnaise, and a few boiled eggs and onions tossed in, it is otherwise every bit the all-American potato salad.

Some of the children give me small gifts to remember them by. Ana gives me a white-and-blue-checked handkerchief onto which she has embroidered a scene with a little rancho. Oscar brings my new sombrero, handmade by his wife. And Edgar's children give me a pouch full of shiny seeds of the corotú. Surrounded by well-wishers, I am amazed to see Francisco approach the school and am further astounded to learn that he has come to Tranquilla just for this event.

He shakes my hand and thanks me. "For all you have done, Maria. Of the Peace Corps Volunteers we have had in the park, you have been one of the most effective. Got things done, you know?" How far Francisco and I have come—from distrust to respect, then even a professional friendship, after a fashion. Gabi arrives with the baby and lets me hold him for a few minutes as I continue chatting with Francisco.

The children drag the desks and tables from the classroom. Señor Lorenzo pulls out his accordion and sets up in a corner with his loosely organized folk band consisting tonight of Manuel and Gabi's oldest son. We dance as a group, children, men, and women together, until dusk. I try to catch Francisco's eye and think it would be fitting to dance together. But under the circumstances, and especially with Ethan absent, it would be inappropriate and awkward. So, the sun sets, we move the furniture back, and I go home.

Tomorrow, INRENARE will send a boat to pick me up on a beautiful, quiet morning. I will climb in with my pack and motor away from Tranquilla for the last time. I will join Ethan at the research station for a few weeks before we leave Panamá for good. Tonight, though, I turn down the kerosene lamp and drift off to the last of the scuffles and giggling from the school up the hill. My dance with this village feels unfinished. The night closes around my heart of palms.

Epilogue

It was a few years following my Peace Corps service that I first heard the term "paper park." All over the world, places like Chagres National Park are designated as "protected areas." These places have one thing in common: governments declared them for noble conservation purposes, but with little regard for the needs of the rural poor. A case in point, Chagres was established to secure the water supply needed to keep the Panama Canal operational and to secure the drinking water supply for Panama City and Colón.

The activities that can be conducted within areas designated as bioreserves are restricted in the name of a greater societal benefit, such as watershed protection. But such benefits come at a cost to local communities, which are often relocated outside the park boundaries. Although this was not Tranquilla's fate, its residents daily faced the tension of choosing between access to their traditional livelihoods, which involved using the park's resources, or complying with the park regulations.

Prior to my time in Chagres, my only experience with national parks had been the US model: seize the land, mark the boundaries, install a Visitor Center and other amenities, and charge an entry fee. The Chagres boundary was nothing more than an invisible line drawn around nearly five hundred square miles of tropical forest. This imaginary line also encompassed the daily lives of some three thousand people. In what sense was this area protected? And from whom?

Reflecting on my years in Chagres has helped me come to terms with modern conservation's shift in focus. Today's conservation movement in the United States is increasingly concerned with the relationships between people and nature. Leaving behind the concept of saving untouched wilderness is an ongoing process, painful on the one hand and, frankly, a relief on the other. After all, when it comes down to it, don't we *all* want to be in relationship with nature, not just an occasional visitor to it? Emma Marris captures the nature of the conservation movement's identity crisis beautifully in her recent book, *Rambunctious Garden*.

On the other hand, the notion of a pristine place that remains unspoiled by humans has an allure that will be tough to shake. Such notions are rooted in a conservationist and literary tradition that spans more than a century. The idea of a nature we are not actively using other than to enjoy and treasure gives the illusion of bounty and spaciousness. Our home has extra rooms.

My passion for ecological restoration was ignited during those years in Panamá. The science and practice of restoration is a hopeful lens through which to view the relationships of people with their environment. Humans have messed things up. We can never put things back the way we found them, but restoration—sowing seeds, planting seedlings, pulling weeds, diversifying habitats—can help us make improvements to our fixer-upper planet. Moreover, toward what end are we trying to restore things? Nine times out of ten, humans benefit from restoring a function, process, or habitat. We work on healing nature and in the process save ourselves.

Often we get it wrong. For example, the native range of leucaena, one of the tree species I planted in Chagres, is from southern Mexico to northern Central America, not to Panamá. A Google search today on "*Leucaena leucocephala* invasive" returns approximately thirty-two thousand hits. Although it is unclear whether leucaena is choking out native trees in Panamá, it is considered a weedy pest in many areas outside its native range, including Florida, Texas, and California. The very characteristics that make it appealing for agroforestry—rapid growth, few diseases, early seeding—are qualities that make it as problematically invasive as paja mala itself. With the best of intentions, and the encouragement of my counterpart Panamanian agency, I served as a vector for introducing aggressive weeds into a national park.

On the bright side, some of our efforts in the early 1990s continue today and show real promise. For example, a team of researchers from McGill University in Montreal, working with indigenous peoples of Panamá, published several papers on conserving native palms and medicinal plants. Between 1998 and 2003, Catherine Potvin and her colleagues developed propagation methods for four native palm species. They worked with several native villages to reintroduce all four species and also developed management and conservation guidelines that factored in traditional uses. I take great satisfaction in knowing that Potvin and her crew furthered palm restoration and conservation work in Panamá, albeit through an entirely independent effort. These folks did in a systematic and scientifically rigorous fashion what I haphazardly attempted decades ago. Scientific breakthroughs in the control of paja mala have also been encouraging.

From 2001 through the present, work conducted largely in conjunction with the Smithsonian Tropical Research Institute has demonstrated the effectiveness of shading and reforestation as ways to reclaim areas invaded by paja. In this case, I have to wonder if it is in any way possible that my early work planted the seed for this research. It seems far-fetched, and there is no way to be sure. But I did present preliminary methods and results from my demonstration plot to a group of Smithsonian scientists in 1992. Although some audience members seemed receptive, one scientist in particular was dismissive of my approach. I had not done a comprehensive literature review, and I was just "out there trying stuff," as he put it. Indeed, being "out there trying stuff" pretty well sums up the Peace Corps experience. Regardless, it is affirming that this technique, piloted so long ago by a handful of Peace Corps Volunteers, has been vetted by some of the finest researchers in the field of ecology.

Another bright spot is the ongoing conservation work of Sustainable Harvest International (SHI). It is a thrill to see the strides SHI is making in finding conservation solutions that benefit both people and nature: tank rice, organic gardening, microloan banks, and more sophisticated wood-conserving stoves are among the recent projects.

If there is one thing climate change, the dead zone in the Gulf of Mexico, and atmospheric deposition of mercury have done for humanity, it's to make it perfectly clear that our actions pack a collective punch. Our daily, individual activities—both good and bad—impact other humans and nature all over the world. The only silver lining of what we have wreaked is the comfort of knowing that as individuals we are by definition part of nature—whether we know it, or like it, or not.

My formative years in conservation were spent living in a final frontier of sorts. Chagres was a skirmish zone in a people versus nature border dispute. On the surface of my Peace Corps service I was conscious of the survival skills I was developing, but something deeper was also going on. Despite my obliviousness at the time, my Peace Corps stint continues to be the most influential experience of my professional career. Those years got me thinking about how to make a human-caused problem better, but I was limited by my lack of education and expertise.

In the last few months of my Peace Corps service, I applied to graduate school and was accepted to the University of Minnesota's forestry program in the spring of 1993. Ethan and I returned to the United States to do what we naïvely assumed to be "real" conservation, leaving the paper park phenomenon behind. We thought things would be so much easier in our own country, where conservation means conservation. This naïveté lasted approximately two minutes in northern Minnesota, where forest conservation and restoration are bound up in a legacy of exploitative logging dating from the early 1900s, as well as today's intensive forest management, and a powerful timber industry. I switched to the study of northern conifers, rather than palms, but the issues of exploitation and incompatible land management transferred perfectly. Chagres by another name.

Twenty years later, Ethan and I are in the midst of planning a return trip to Panamá with our six-year-old daughter. We'll be there within a few months, and I am nervous about what we'll find there. We have no illusions that people and nature have miraculously achieved a peaceful coexistence within Chagres National Park. But has progress been made on that front? Is Tranquilla still there? Do any of our projects persist? Most importantly, will the people remember us; will they welcome us? We are daunted by the prospect of returning to the scene of experiences that were often difficult, painful, and tedious. But curiosity has gotten the better of us—as it did the first time.

Resources

The following online resources may be of interest to readers who want to learn more about organizations currently working at the nexus of conservation and social issues in Panamá:

Asociación Nacional para la Conservación de la Naturaleza (ANCON) (National Association for the Conservation of Nature)

This nonprofit has a biodiversity conservation mission and was founded in 1985. http://www.ancon.org

International Palm Society

Although its activities are not limited to Panamá, the International Palm Society is a great resource for learning more about the propagation, conservation, and uses of palms. http://www.palms.org

Native Future

Founded in 2003, Native Future works with the Wounaan, Ñgäbe, and Buglé indigenous people of Panamá to conserve cultures and threatened lands. http://www.nativefuture.org

Neotropical Ecology Laboratory (McGill University)

This team of researchers, led by Dr. Catherine Potvin, did groundbreaking work in the area of "science for empowerment," balancing livelihoods and biodiversity, including propagation methods for native palm species. They continue to work with indigenous groups in Panamá, with a current focus on whether traditional uses of forests can enhance carbon storage. http://biology.mcgill.ca/faculty/potvin/livelihood_biodiv.html

Peace Corps

The Peace Corps's Panamá program is alive and well and continues to have an environmental and sustainable agriculture component. http://www.peacecorps.gov/learn/wherepc/centralamerica/panama

Planting Empowerment

Planting Empowerment is a socially responsible forestry company dedicated to growing native tropical hardwoods in partnership with rural communities to provide both social and economic benefits. http://www.plantingempowerment.com

The Nature Conservancy

The Nature Conservancy is the largest nonprofit conservation organization in the world. The Conservancy has programs throughout Central and South America, including Panamá. http://www.nature.org/ourinitiatives/regions/centralamerica/panama/index.htm

Smithsonian Tropical Research Institute (STRI)

Based in Panamá, STRI has research programs and conservation initiatives throughout the tropics around the world. http://www.stri.si.edu/english/conservation/index.php

Sustainable Harvest International (SHI)

Founded in 1997, SHI works with families in rural farming communities toward finding alternatives to slash-and-burn agriculture. www.sustainableharvest.org

Unión Campesina del Lago Alajuela (UCLA)
(Farmer's Union of Lake Alajuela)

Two decades later, UCLA continues its work on improving quality of life through the use of sustainable farming practices. I was ecstatic to find it

online and to learn that beekeeping remains central to its programs. http://
www.ucla.pymeparquechagres.org

Meredith W. Cornett: Memoir and More

Finally, my own website has additional resources, including updates
to *Heart of Palms* and photos of Tranquilla and its people. http://www
.meredithwcornett.com

Bibliography

Condit, Richard, Rolando Pérez, and Nefertaris Daguerre. *Trees of Panama and Costa Rica*. Princeton, NJ: Princeton University Press, 2011.
    A useful reference consulted to verify facts related to native tree species, their distribution, and the like throughout the text for *Heart of Palms*.

Hooper, Elaine, Richard Condit, and Pierre Legendre. "Response of 20 Native Tree Species to Reforestation Strategies for Abandoned Farmland in Panama." *Ecological Applications* 12 (2002): 1626–41.
    Research by this group suggests we were on the right track with our early attempts to reclaim areas overrun by paja mala, particularly in the selection of albizia as a shade tree.

Hooper, Elaine, Pierre Legendre, and Richard Condit. "Barriers to Forest Regeneration of Deforested and Abandoned Land in Panama." *Journal of Applied Ecology* 42, no. 6 (2005): 1165–74.
    This second research paper by these scientists affirms the general approach they call "facilitated succession," but the extreme measures we took in cutting and uprooting paja mala may have been unnecessary. They also suggest a focus on fruit producers to attract birds and mammals that will in turn disperse the seed.

John F. Kennedy Presidential Library and Museum. "JFK in History: Peace Corps." Accessed January 25, 2013. http://www.jfklibrary.org/JFK/JFK-in-History/Peace-Corps.aspx.
    Concentrates on the life and legacy of John F. Kennedy, with a substantial section on the establishment of the Peace Corps. Consulted in preparation of the introduction for *Heart of Palms*.

Kim, Taek Joo, Florencia Montagnini, and Daisy Dent. "Rehabilitating Abandoned Pastures in Panama: Control of the Invasive Exotic Grass, *Saccharum spontaneum* L., Using Artificial Shade Treatments." *Journal of Sustainable Forestry* 26, no. 3 (2008): 192–93.

This article suggests that the density of *Saccharum spontaneum* decreases as the density of canopy tree crowns increases.

Koster, R. M., and Guillermo Sánchez. *In the Time of the Tyrants: Panama 1968–1990*. New York: Norton, 1990.

Information about Manuel Noriega's rule and the military leaders preceding him was drawn in part from this reference and used in the introduction of *Heart of Palms*.

Marris, Emma. *Rambunctious Garden: Saving Nature in a Post-Wild World*. New York: Bloomsbury, 2011.

My current thinking about nature, people, and wilderness has been influenced by this elegant book, as reflected particularly in the epilogue of *Heart of Palms*.

Pérez, Rolando, and Richard Condit. "Tree Atlas of Panamá." Smithsonian Tropical Research Institute, Center for Tropical Forest Science. http://ctfs.arnarbharvard.edu/webatlas/maintreeatlas.php.

Consulted frequently for cross-checking my notes on the identification, life history, and distribution of several Panamanian trees, shrubs, and palms throughout the text of *Heart of Palms*.

Potvin, Catherine, Rogelio Cansari, Jane Hutton, Inocencio Caisamo, and Bonarge Pacheco. "Preparation for Propagation: Understanding Germination of Giwa (*Astrocaryum standleyanum*), Wagara (*Sabal mauritiiformis*), and Eba (*Socratea exorrhiza*) for Future Cultivation." *Biodiversity and Conservation* 12 (2003): 2161–71.

This paper centers on work conducted in the Darién region of Panama. I was heartened to learn about the degree to which these scientists involved local indigenous communities in the sustainable management of native palms they use in different facets of their daily lives.

Werner, David, Carol Thuman, and Jane Maxwell. *Donde no hay doctor: Una guía para los campesinos que viven lejos de los centros médicos* [*Where There Is No Doctor: A Village Health Care Handbook*]. Palo Alto: La Fundación Hesperian, 1973.

This is the Peace Corps–issued medical handbook referenced throughout *Heart of Palms*. Full of practical first-aid advice and clear illustrations, it has been translated into more than one hundred languages and has sold more than one million copies.